Praise

Wisdom in a Traffic Jam

"In business you sometimes come across a person who runs both their business and their life with focus and determination. The result is a force to be reckoned with!' Angella Luyk is just such a person. Her drive and commitment to succeed leave a wide path through the woods for anyone similarly motivated to achieve success themselves."

— **Martin F. Palumbo**s, CLU, ChFC, CFP
PS&E, LLC Plan to Prosper

"Angella Luyk has become a compelling and powerful force in both my life and the life of our Rochester business community. Her positive outlook, can-do attitude and unwavering commitment to the highest ethical standards are an absolute How to...for not only creating and operating a business, but also living a positive, contributing life of meaning. Her well-deserved ethics awards have become a beacon to our community on the value of doing things the right way."

— **Alan R. Ziegler**, Futures Funding Corp.

"Most business books talk about theory and experiences that are not very hands on to small business owners. Angella has reflected not only on her own experiences, mistakes and learnings but included those from a broad spectrum of different small business owners. When starting and running a small business nothing goes as planned, and we get squeezed from all directions just trying to operate and succeed day to day. Reading this book will provide valuable insight into avoiding the pitfalls and building on the successes of others to get out of the small business "traffic jam" and into the "express lane" of small business success."

— **Jerry Elman**, Owner Schoen Place Auto

"*While most authors just lay out the information like some cold heartless computer, Angella forms the information like building a pyramid, one step at a time. While making the reading of information easy to understand, she creates questions the new business owner might not think to ask.*"

— **Kevin Kreitzberg**, Entrepreneur

"*I read Wisdom in a Traffic Jam, and followed the advice on Goal Setting. I set a goal to bring in 5 new clients; I was amazed when I received 7 new clients. Angella's strategies work. This is a must have book for anyone looking to succeed in life.*"

— **Josh Grover**, Personal Trainer

Wisdom in a Traffic Jam

The secrets nobody tells you about owning an AMAZING successful business

Angella Luyk

NEW YORK

Wisdom in a Traffic Jam
The secrets nobody tells you about owning an AMAZING successful business

by Angella Luyk
© 2011 Angella Luyk. All rights reserved.

Disclaimer: The Publisher and the Author make no representations or warranties with respect to the accuracy or completeness of the contents of this work and specifically disclaim all warranties, including without limitation warranties of fitness for a particular purpose. No warranty may be created or extended by sales or promotional materials. The advice and strategies contained herein may not be suitable for every situation. This work is sold with the understanding that the Publisher is not engaged in rendering legal, accounting, or other professional services. If professional assistance is required, the services of a competent professional person should be sought. Neither the Publisher nor the Author shall be liable for damages arising herefrom. The fact that an organization or website is referred to in this work as a citation and/or a potential source of further information does not mean that the Author or the Publisher endorses the information the organization or website may provide or recommendations it may make. Further, readers should be aware that internet websites listed in this work may have changed or disappeared between when this work was written and when it is read.

ISBN 978-1-60037-976-5 Paperback
ISBN 978-1-60037-977-2 EPub Version
Library of Congress Control Number: 2011924065

Published by:

MORGAN JAMES PUBLISHING
The Entrepreneurial Publisher
5 Penn Plaza, 23rd Floor
New York City, New York 10001
(212) 655-5470 Office
(516) 908-4496 Fax
www.MorganJamesPublishing.com

**Cover Illustration
and Design by:**
JanMarie Gallagher

Editing by:
Emily Carpenter

Interior Design by:
Bonnie Bushman
bbushman@bresnan.net

In an effort to support local communities, raise awareness and funds, Morgan James Publishing donates one percent of all book sales for the life of each book to Habitat for Humanity.
Get involved today, visit
www.HelpHabitatForHumanity.org.

This book is dedicated to a few special people who have seen me through a lot. First I must say thank you to my husband, Harry, who has stood by me through thick and thin, I love you dearly. My sister Sam, who I may not speak to every day, but I know that she is there for me, and I for her. A special thanks to Emily and baby John Warner who made this process so much fun. And finally to my partner in crime, Becky. Each of these people has given me the courage and encouragement to keep going. I will forever be grateful to them.

Thank you.

Contents

Preface

Ever since I was a little girl, I have wanted to write a book. Most of my childhood was spent reading books and as I entered adulthood my thirst for knowledge only became stronger. I always have a book with me. The day I discovered business books was the most important day of my life. Here was a whole new world for me to explore. I never planned to be a business owner; I originally wanted to be a lawyer until I realized that I would have to memorize hundreds of cases. So I decided that I would go into the teaching field. After all, I loved helping people. Unfortunately, I couldn't sit still long enough and I hated being "trapped" in a classroom all day. I often think I may have a little ADD (Attention Deficit Disorder). I am constantly on the move. Most things hold my attention for only a short period of time before I am off to the next project. Being a business owner seemed to be a good fit. You wear so many different hats that you never get bored. Things are constantly changing; problems need to be solved quickly. You are kept on your toes.

The only problem was that I had no idea how to run a business. My background was in psychology and teaching. I turned to books to help educate me. I quickly found the For Dummies series of books. There is huge collection of them on every topic imaginable. You can learn anything from how to create a business plan, to human resource issues, to how to manage stress, and boy do you need that one!

1

As I grew my business, more and more people would ask me how I did it. Did I have some secrets I could share with them? Could I offer them some words of wisdom? In 2006 I became ill and for the next few years I would battle an unknown illness that would put me in the hospital on and off. I was confined to my house for weeks at a time. Thankfully my business continued to grow and to the amazement of my doctors and friends, I kept a happy and positive attitude. I would have the nurses in ICU (Intensive Care Unit) laughing. At one point I had to be intubated. This is not a pleasant experience. I lost four days of my life. Throughout this whole experience I learned a lot about my business and my employees. To this day I have still not been diagnosed, but continue to keep a positive attitude.

I now was armed with book knowledge and practical experience. People came to me for even more advice. They wanted to know how I could stay so happy while dealing with an undiagnosed illness and a bad economy. My business continued to grow despite all the setbacks my health was causing. The answer is simple: I don't know any other way to operate. Yes, life can be difficult at times and I don't like being sick, but you know, someone is always worse off than me. I could be battling cancer or have a failing business. I also have the loving support of my husband and some really great friends. Friends who you will meet as you read this book. My hope is that you will read this, take some knowledge away, and better your life.

Remember no matter how bad it gets there is someone who has it worse than you. My friend Dwayne sums it up nicely when he says "You can continue to complain about it and you will lose friends or you can shut up, suck it up, and do something about it."

As you can see I decided to shut up and do something about it. I take it one day at a time, one idea or inspiration at a time. As you can see from my book cover I get my best ideas when I am sitting in traffic. Most people become frustrated, they want to be moving, and I see it as a few moments to reflect on my day. As a business owner you are going to have to find your special place to reflect; perhaps for you it will be in the shower, or when you are in a restaurant waiting for someone. Take those few moments, and breathe. It does get easier.

I want to say a special thanks to my friend Lisa Riggi and her daughter Jess. Without their help and support this book would not be possible. They both make great editors. Special thanks also goes out to my two doctors, Dr. Minnella and Dr. Bingeman for planting the seed that I could write this book.

Enjoy!

Angella

1
Have a Plan

You have made the decision to start your own business. You are ready to take a leap of faith and go out on your own. Only problem is, you may be wondering: "Where do I start?" Starting a business can be scary. There is so much to do and know; who can you turn to? Are there resources to help you? My hope is that as you read this book, I can help provide some of these answers.

The Idea

The first thing you need to do is ask yourself, "Why do you want to start a business?" Are you good at something? If so, what is it about this particular something that interests you? (We will talk about the importance of being passionate in a later chapter). If your answer to this question is: 1) you're bored with your current job; 2) you hate your current boss/company; or 3) you just got laid off and have nothing else to do, then I suggest you rethink your options. The biggest myth is that being a business owner is easy. You get to come and go as you please. Unfortunately, when starting a business it isn't that easy. In the beginning, you have no free time. You will eat, sleep, and think about your business 24 hours a day/7 days a week.

When I started my business, I would network during the day, and do the actual work in the evenings. Weekends were my time to catch up on paperwork, create plans for my business, and do my household chores. I spent many late nights paying bills or putting together new proposals. In the beginning you don't have a lot of money or people to outsource some of the little things to, so as the owner, you get to do everything. In time, as your business grows, you will have more money and people to help you. You should always be hands on, but you can back off a bit.

The Plan

The second thing to do is to create a plan. Think of this as your road map. Believe me when I tell you it will change; you will come across many detours and road blocks. You may even change your business's product or service to better suit your clients' needs. When I started my janitorial company, my plan was to only clean offices, until a client asked me to get them some paper and plastic products. Soon, I started offering these products to all of my clients. By the end of the year I saw a 20% increase in revenue. I was already going to the buildings so it was not an imposition to make more money. A few months later I added hard floor care and carpet care services. By adding these services, I was able to keep my competition out. My clients like writing one check to one vendor. If I hadn't been willing to add paper products and floor care, I may have lost clients. I definitely would have lost out on added revenue. The plan you put in place for your business should be used as a guide. Change is always going to happen, you must be willing to work with it, and grow.

Your business may be a bit different than what you expect, but I encourage you to keep an open mind. Be flexible and grow with your clients. If you become too rigid and set in your ways, you may lose some great opportunities.

Creating Your Dream

When creating your plan you also want to consider what type of business you are going to have. What I mean is, are you going to be a corporation (there are about five different types) or a DBA (Doing Business As). Each type has different positives and negatives. The best thing to do is to contact a business attorney, and discuss what is best for your needs and where you want to go with your business. You need to take a moment to decide if you are going to have a partner or partners. This is fine if that is what you want to do, just be sure to clearly plan and define each person's roll. For example: two people cannot be writing business checks. One person should be responsible for this. I'm not saying you can't have checks and balances, because you should. You want to make sure everyone is clear on their responsibilities. Take the time to write these down so you will have them to refer to in times of doubt. Just as your business will change, so will each person's roll in your business. People will come in and out of your business. The key is to find out each person's strengths, and have them help you by putting them into a role that suits their talents. Their roles will change. Over time, your sales person could become your vice president. Let these people grow with you. You will meet a lot of business professionals that can help guide you and your business. Be open to their ideas and suggestions; they are, after all, the professionals.

Speaking of business professionals, you want to contact a good CPA (Certified Public Accountant). These people are different from regular accountants, who may do personal taxes, as they keep up to date on the many changing tax laws. Ideally, you will meet with them once a quarter to ensure that you are on the right track with your taxes. When I first met my accountant he helped get the ball rolling with some really helpful advice. For example, he helped explain to us the different things we could write off versus what we could not.

When you first meet with your attorney, CPA, or any professional who is going to help you grow your business, don't be afraid to ask them lots of questions. You are essentially interviewing them for a position in your company. If they don't prove to you that they can help you, walk away. You may be saying to yourself that you don't know anyone. Ask around. See who other business people are using. Are they happy? Do they feel that their relationship is adding value to their company? Be careful of the people who tell you my good friend does this on the side. He charges half the going rate or something close to this. You get what you pay for. Just as in your business you want to offer the best service at the best price: you want anyone you work with to do the same.

After you have assembled your team of professionals you can next decide who your clients are going to be. You may do this step before you hire your team, and that is fine. Just be comfortable when deciding who your client is and deciding what your niche market is. This may also change over time, but you need to start somewhere. The best advice I can offer here is to start out small. You can expand over time. Don't be afraid to tell a potential client that you can't help them if they don't fit your niche. To over expand too quickly can ruin your reputation.

Your Market

When deciding on your target market, ask yourself the following questions:

- How big a company can I work with? Small, medium, or large businesses?

- What area do I want to cover? A 100 mile radius? The whole state?

- How much payroll/expenses can I pay out before I get reimbursed?

Make sure that you can deliver whatever you promise to a client. For example, if you make jewelry by hand and you know that you can only produce 20 pieces of jewelry a week, you probably would want to work with a small boutique versus a big chain store. When I started out, my niche was small offices, which I defined as offices with fewer than 20 employees. Over time, as I perfected my business, I was able to expand and work with medium-sized offices. I have been offered the big 20-story office buildings and I have said no every time. I don't mass hire employees. In order to clean those types of buildings that is what I would have to do. This goes against what I wanted to offer. In time I may change my mind. One of the good things about owning your business is that you're able to make those decisions.

Unfortunately, you have to make a lot of other decisions as well. Sometimes, it can be overwhelming. I can't stress enough to seek out professional help whenever possible. It may cost you a little more up front, but could save you a lot more over time.

Employees vs. Subcontractors

After you have decided who your prefect client is going to be, it's time to decide if you are going to hire employees (we will talk about hiring employees in more detail in a later chapter) subcontractors, or do all of the work yourself. A subcontractor is someone who has a business of their own, but does some work for you. They typically have their own business cards, have decided on their own rate to charge, and have set up their own hours that they will work. An employee is someone who works directly for you: you tell them exactly what hours you want them to work and set their salary. They may negotiate with you for a higher pay rate or different hours, but you ultimately have the final say. It is best to check with your CPA to ensure you are following all the proper guidelines.

Your Office Space

Now is the time to give some thought to where you will do business. Are you going to have an office, a storefront, a commercial building, or work from a home office? Many people have chosen to go the route of working from home. There used to be a stigma on "home based businesses." Slowly, with the changes in the economy and more people getting laid off, there is an upswing in working from home. The U.S. Small Business Administration presents an award to the Home-Based Business Champion of the Year. I like working from home because if I get an idea in the middle of the night I don't have to get in the car and drive to an office to work. I can be in my pajamas and get work done at any hour. Now the downside to this is that some people get distracted by being at home and don't get much work done. You do have to be rather disciplined to work from home.

Another positive is that if you have a dedicated office in your home you may be able to pay yourself rent and write off some of your utilities. You should check with your CPA for the exact rules and percentages.

If you've decided that you need to rent office space, be prepared that the amount may be higher than if you were to rent an apartment. Commercial leases and utilities are usually higher than their residential equivalent. If you decide to go with a lease, try and have enough money set aside to pay the first six months in the event that your business hits a few bumps in the road. Don't be afraid to try and negotiate the price per month and the terms. They may say no, but they may also say yes. What have you got to lose?

Paying the Bills

Bumps in the road can consist of clients not paying you in a timely fashion. A common misconception that people have is that you get paid every week. Now, I'm not saying that this never happens, but it is rare. Generally, if you are providing a service on a daily basis you will bill them at the end of the month and will be paid anywhere from 30 to 90 days later. If you are providing a one-time service you can ask for a deposit with the remainder due at the time services are finished, however, you may still have to wait 30 days. When you draw up the contract with a potential client you can put the terms in there (we will talk about contracts in a later chapter).

Just because you may not get paid immediately does not mean that your employees or sub-contractors will want to wait to get paid. Part of your plan needs to cover how you are going to pay your bills while waiting to get your money from a client. One of the things that I do is use a business credit card. I found one that pays me back with different reward options. I can choose cash or a gift certificate for a store. I can also choose to pay the bill all at once or through a payment plan over time. Just be careful with the interest rates with credit cards. With the new law, credit card companies now must disclose the amount of interest you will be charged over a year period. This helps to make it a bit easier to plan your payments out. You may decide you want to get a small business loan. Shop around to get the best rate. If you can't get a business credit card or loan you may still be able to secure a loan with your personal guarantee. Be sure and find out the interest rate; is there a penalty for pre-payments? Some banks expect you to keep the loan for a certain amount of time. It could be two, five, or ten years, check with your local bank for their terms. The bank makes money on the long-term interest payments made. If you pay off the loan early before the intended date, the bank loses money. To counteract this, they put prepayment penalties in place. By law, the bank needs to disclose any of these fees before you sign the paperwork. Depending on the state you live in, you usually have three to seven days to decide if you do not want the loan after all. Again, check with your bank for these details, as they may vary.

The Name Game

Let's take a moment to talk about your company name. A few things you want to think about are:

1. Can someone tell what services or products you offer when they hear the company name? (e.g. Joe's Floors: does Joe sell floors, install floors, or clean floors? You might be better off with Joe's Floor Restoration.)

2. Think hard before putting your first name in the company name (e.g. Joe's Floors). Everyone is going to ask if you are Joe. If you want to eventually sell or franchise your business, the new owner may not be named Joe. You will have built your reputation around this particular name that no one wants to buy. You can always use your initials (e.g. JP's Floor Restoration).

3. Keep the name short. If it takes too long to say the name you are going to lose people's attention. For example, "JP's Floor Stripping, Waxing, Restoration and Finishing Services, Inc." will not fit so well on a business card or sign.

When I was deciding on my company name, I played the name game. I knew that I wanted to use the word janitorial, but didn't know what else I was going to put with it. So my husband and I started saying every word we could think of with janitorial. We started by saying *blue* janitorial, *cleaning* janitorial, words that didn't necessarily make sense, but got us thinking. Eventually one of us said *Midnight*

Janitorial, and we both instantly loved it; Midnight Janitorial has been our name ever since.

Focus!

When you are considering a business, pick one product and or service to associate it with. If you are going to be a corporation that represents many businesses you are OK. It is when you are just starting out and have multiple businesses listed on your card or website that people may think, "Can't they decide on what they want to focus on?" I usually do.

Imagine if I stood up and gave my infomercial and said, "I am here to talk about my janitorial company, my photography business and a line of makeup that I created." Someone listening may not understand how each of these things fits together. Have you heard the phrase jack of all trades, master of none? Instead of making me look like I can do a lot of different things well, I come across as looking like since I can't decide what I want to do, I'm just trying a few things out for awhile to see what sticks. The perception is that I won't be doing all of them long term, so using me for any of them may turn out to be a poor investment. Even if you have a company that offers seemingly different services, it's a good idea to only focus on one at a time when giving your infomercial. I could say, "Midnight Janitorial Inc. represents many different businesses to suit all your needs," but then only talk about one particular service. Keep it simple so as to not overwhelm your audience.

The Drive

Remember to make sure that the business product or service that you choose to focus your business on is something that you are truly passionate about. When you love what you do it seems less like work.

If you wake up every day with the attitude that you hate what you are doing, you will fail.

I tend to attract a lot of people to me. They can tell by my positive attitude that I love what I do. I don't mean cleaning toilets. I mean running my business! I love teaching new employees how to do things and talking to potential clients about how we can help them make their life easier. When I'm smiling and happy people want to talk to me, and when they talk to me they get to know who I am. Business is personal. We have probably all heard the saying "It's not what you know, it's who you know." It's also about "who knows you." Just by loving what I do I get to know a lot more people that want to know me too.

You are starting a new journey in your life. Make sure that you're truly passionate about this. You were probably unhappy in your last job; you have the opportunity to be happy now. Go for it!

2
Networking

When starting a business, money is limited. How do you get your name out there without spending a lot? You can network.

The first time I went to a networking event, I thought to myself, "I am going to blow these people away." Oh, how wrong I was! I arrived in these cute white shorts and colored shirt. This outfit was great for a picnic, but not a business networking event. The problem was that I didn't know any better. I walked into the event and instantly realized my mistake. Everyone was in suits or slacks and dress shirts. Too late to turn back; they had already seen me. Later, I realized that had I sat in the parking lot and watched as they walked in, I would have seen how everyone was dressed and could have followed their lead and dressed appropriately.

Introducing Yourself

I walked into the room and instantly froze up. What was I supposed to do? Walk up to these people or wait for them to talk to me? After standing alone for a few minutes I walked up to two people deep in conversation. That was a big mistake. It was very hard for me to insert myself into their conversation. I ended up standing there feeling like an idiot. They wouldn't even look at me! I walked away and found a small group of people, and instantly made eye contact with the person speaking. He finished what he was saying then invited me in the conversation. He introduced himself and the rest of the group and asked who I was. I shook hands with each person as I said my name and repeated theirs. Repeating the name of a person you meet makes it easier to remember. Plus, people love to hear their own name. As each person was speaking to me, they explained to me what they did and the name of their company. I noticed how they did this smoothly and in a short amount of time. When it came to be my turn I couldn't think of anything to say. I was so nervous that I just started rambling. It was horrible! How was anyone going to take me seriously or give me their business if I couldn't even tell them what I did?

Later I learned that what I had heard from each person was called an infomercial. This is a commercial about who you are and what you do. You can have multiple infomercials based on your audience. You want to create a message that will interest people into scheduling a meeting. You are not trying to close the deal at this point. You just want them interested enough that when you call them they will answer the telephone, or better yet, they will call you first.

Opening Your Infomercial

The question then becomes: What goes into your infomercial? Start with your name and your company name. That is the easy part. The body of your message and who your audience is will help to determine what else you say. Grab their attention by talking about something that will help them. What is their biggest problem? How can you help them to solve it? My friend Lisa owns a company that offers per diem office assistance. If she is in a roomful of sales people, her message is going to be different from a roomful of small business owners. For the salespeople, she may focus on how she can put out a mass mailing of letters to potential new clients. She may say something like: "Ask me how I can introduce you to thousands of potential clients by typing a letter for you and using your database to send a personal introduction to all of your contacts. Stop wasting time doing the little stuff that I can do for you and start closing more deals!"

If she is talking in front of small business owners, she may talk about the tedious task of filing. Lisa may ask the question, "How many of us have stacks of paperwork that need filing and the piles just never seem to get smaller? No matter how much time we set aside to get to it, it just never seems like it is enough." She may then go on to explain how she can come in for a few hours a week and take care of this. Because she charges per job, they would be saving money by not having to hire someone on a full- or part-time basis to do the job; especially when they may not have enough work to keep this person busy all the time.

Lisa is listening to what people do and tailoring her infomercial to best suit them. Find out what someone's "pain" is, solve it for them, and they will have an interest in you. If you don't have time before you speak to find out what everyone does, keep your message more broad and generic. Lisa, for example, may just explain that she owns a company that is here to help with your office needs. She may say something like, "When you can't afford a full-time assistant you can hire me per diem; on a daily, weekly, or monthly basis. You decide how much you need me."

During Your Infomercial

Here you can offer any discounts or specials you have going on. Perhaps this is your one year anniversary; let people know this. Another option is to ask for new business. You need to be careful here to make sure you explain who your ideal client is. Back to Lisa as an example; she may say "I am looking for the small business

owner with less than 30 employees who needs a little help around
the office sending out mass mailings, updating a database, or filing
paperwork." She is being very specific in what she wants. You don't
want people giving you leads that you are not interested in (we will
discuss leads later in this chapter).

Closing Your Infomercial

Now comes the ending of your infomercial. This is where you
wrap it all up by repeating your name and your company name.
Give them a way to contact you, perhaps your website or a phone
number. Now is also the time to say your "catch phrase." This is a
few words that people will remember you by. In just a few seconds,
your catch phrase helps explain who you are and what you stand
for. You can also use this when people ask you what you do. I own
a commercial cleaning company so I often will say, "And remember,
at Midnight Janitorial we are cleaning up Rochester one office at a
time." It is clear and precise. You know I clean offices, commercial
buildings, and not houses.

End your infomercial with a call to action and a sense of urgency.
Lisa might say something like: "Stop thinking about getting help
with your office chores and call me now: before your next busy
season arrives."

The hard part of your infomercial is saying everything you want to
say in a short amount of time. You will be offered anywhere between
10 seconds to 60 seconds with 30 seconds being the norm. Yes, I said
30 seconds! I know you are panicked, how can you possibly get your
message across in such a short time? Would you believe me if I told
you that most people stop paying attention after about 5 seconds? If
you look around you will see people writing grocery lists, looking out
the window, or worse, picking lint off of their suits!

Presentation

How can you avoid this? First, start by standing up (if you are originally sitting). You talk from lower in your diaphragm; when sitting you are pushing down and won't be able to use the most oxygen. Stand tall and let your voice project loud and clear. Do not talk in a monotone voice (again, boring)! Instead, try some vocal variety. Be interactive with your audience. Ask them a question to get their attention. You may say, "Are we all enjoying the great weather outside?" Then pause (let them answer you) and then start your infomercial.

If you are nervous about talking in front of people, you can practice. Gather a few friends that you trust and present your infomercial to them. Ask them to critique you. Try not to be offended if they say that you need to make changes. Some questions you can ask them are:

- Did you understand what I do? If so, please tell me.
- Did I speak too fast?
- Did I speak clearly?
- Could you hear me?
- Is there anything that you would change?

To take it a step further, you could video tape yourself and watch the video. Take notes and critique the video as if someone else is speaking. Videotaping yourself also works well when you have to give a presentation or sales pitch. There is nothing wrong with writing out your infomercial and reading it. This may help you feel more comfortable until you start to get the hang of it. You can write out bullet points and just glance down or you can write it out word for word. Do what is comfortable for you. The more you give your infomercial, the easier it gets.

Referrals

An infomercial is essentially a plea for a referral or a lead. When talking with people, do not be afraid to ask for what you want. People want to help you, but if they don't know what you want, they can't help you. Don't waste their time, or yours, on business that you don't want. Be as specific as possible, and make sure to ask them what they are looking for as well.

Once you receive a lead, call your new prospect immediately. Prompt follow up shines a favorable light on both you and the person that referred you. Regardless of whether or not the prospect turns into new business, always send a thank you right away to the person that referred you (we will discuss the many ways to say thank you later in the book). Many companies have successful referral programs, offering discounts or money to people who make referrals that turn into paying customers.

Equally important to how you receive a referral, is how you give a referral. Nothing is worse than a fake, or cold, referral. This is when you give out a name and say, "I know so and so and they may be looking for your service." You haven't called your referral to ask if you can give their information out or if they are in need of this service. It's OK to do this occasionally, but make sure that you explain to the person that you aren't sure if this person is in need of their services or not, but they are more than welcome to give them a call. It is better to give nothing than to give a fake referral. Word will get around and soon no one will take you seriously. When you first start networking you won't have a lot of contacts built up and that is OK. Just be honest if someone asks you for a specific referral. Tell them I don't know anyone that needs your service right now, but if I meet someone, I will gladly give them your name. Have you ever heard of paying it forward? This is where you help someone and expect nothing in return. The belief is that good things will happen to you later on. If someone gives you a referral, do not feel as if you have to give them one back. If you can, great! But it is not necessary. Just give good referrals whenever possible.

The ultimate type of referral is a warm, or hot, referral. This is when you give someone as much information as possible including multiple ways to contact the prospect, such as email, phone number, and a website address. It's also helpful to be clear about someone's preference in how they like to be contacted. I am personally better at responding to emails, yet a phone call may take awhile for me to return. Whenever possible, contact the person and let them know that your friend will be calling them. This is called a warm lead. The person being contacted has some idea of what is going on. If you do not call the person first, then it is considered a cold lead. A hot lead is when you call the person first, and they have already agreed that they would like the service before they are contacted by the person you are referring to them. Be sure and follow up with the person you gave the lead to. Ask them how it went, and how you can improve your referrals to them in the future.

Remember when giving a referral, that you are putting your reputation on the line. If the person you are referring does not meet your high standards or work ethic, don't give their name out. Even though you can't control what the referral will do, you will still be held accountable and it may affect your reputation either negatively or positively. The idea is to come out looking like the referral hero, not the villain.

Business Cards

Now that you have listened to their infomercial and given yours, what's next? Exchange the all-important business cards! The business card is what I like to call your passport into the other person's business. This is what they remember you by. What goes into a good business card? The front should have your company name, logo, your name, and contact information. Contact information should be all the ways that people may contact you such as office phone, cell phone, website, email, and social media sites. Make it as easy as possible for people to contact you. You may also want to have your picture. A picture makes the card more personal, and also makes it easier for people to remember and recognize you.

The biggest mistake that people make in designing business cards is forgetting to use the back. This is a blank canvas for you to do anything with. For instance, listing the services you offer will help you when you have less than 60 seconds to tell someone you just met about what you do. Even if you have more time, people will still forget without a reminder. If you list your services, you don't have to worry about it. Other options are to offer a discount or coupon on the back. List the awards you have won that differentiate you from your competition (we will be discussing awards later in the book). Putting a tip calculator on the back gives people a reason to keep your card handy. The following pages show three examples of business cards that use both sides.

Angella Luyk   (585) 414-6960
Angella@midnightjanitorial.com   Fax: (585) 342-5609

www.midnightjanitorial.com
2009 (National) American Ethics Award Recipient
2008 Rochester Business Ethics Award Recipient
Full Service Commercial Janitorial Company
• professional office cleaning
• strip and wax
• paper and plastic products available
• certified carpet cleaning, over 15 certifications
from IICRC

I've listed our website address, awards we've received, and additional services that we offer to the back of my card.

Kevin uses the back of his card to entice people to give him referrals by passing along his card and lists additional services offered.

SCHOEN PLACE
AUTO

Jerry Elman
Owner

office **(585) 381 1970** | 319 East Chestnut Street
www.SchoenPlaceAuto.com | East Rochester, NY 14445

**Taking stress and uncertainty
out of car repairs since 1971**

Recipient of the **2010 Rochester Business Ethics Award**

cell **(585) 737 2737**
fax **(585) 385 9127**

Jerry.Elman@SchoenPlaceAuto.com

*Jerry uses the back of his card to share his car repair
philosophy, and lists additional ways to contact him.*

What color will your card be? Make your card stand out! People usually go with plain white. Personally, I think this is boring. I chose my doctor because she had purple business cards. I thought to myself, "Here is a woman who has a bit of flair." It may be tempting to use a different shape, such as a house or a paint brush, depending on the industry; however, I don't recommend this. Most people carry a business card holder that fits the standard-size business card. If your card doesn't fit, it may get lost or thrown away. Stick with a solid color for the background to make it stand out.

Now that you have your great new business cards, how do you give them away? Who gets a card? When I hand them to new people I give them two cards and say, "Here is one card for you and one for your friend." You will notice people thinking about who they can give the other card to. You have planted a seed in their mind. Plus when you give them only one card, if they give it away, how will they contact you? Don't give them a stack unless they specifically ask you for a bunch of cards. Remember to ask them for two of their business cards.

Before you end the conversation try and set up a time to meet for coffee or lunch. This is when you will really sell yourself and your product. Continue to read on to learn about making the meeting date and following up.

Follow-up: The 3 Rule!

The day has arrived for your coffee or lunch meeting. You have chosen a location close to your prospective client's location (you don't want to inconvenience them and should make it as easy as possible for them to get there). Make sure that you arrive a minimum of fifteen minutes early so that you won't be running late or out of breath. By arriving early you can catch your breath and take a moment. You also can get the best place to sit; there is nothing worse than having to scramble for a seat. When your guest arrives, stand up and greet them. Offer to get them a coffee or water and then go and order it for them. This will give them an opportunity to catch their breath and organize their thoughts. When you return with their drink, make small talk so that they have a chance to take a sip. Ask them if they found the place okay or mention what a great/bad day the weather turned out to be. When you feel your guest is settled in, ask them open-ended questions about their business to get the conversation started.

Before this meeting you should have done some research about the person you are going to meet. Find out who a great client will be for them. Familiarize yourself with their website. This information will make it easier to start and maintain a conversation. You want to control the flow and direction. An opening you may want to ask is, "How did you get into your business?" People love to hear themselves talk and to talk about themselves. As they tell you their story you can insert little tidbits about yourself. People don't want to be sold. They want to be educated. How can you help them solve their problem by partnering with your service or product?

Always end your meeting on a positive note. Perhaps you can say, "I will give you a call and follow up." When do you call them? The next day? A week later? You don't want to seem too pushy or too eager. Have you ever noticed that things seem to happen in threes? Recently I learned that a good friend of mine is pregnant. I was so happy for her as they had been trying for a long time. A few days later I received an email from a colleague on a non-profit board that I serve on saying that she would be resigning from the board because she was pregnant. As you can guess, I was out networking and ran into another friend who was pregnant. This is three people in a short time that I knew where pregnant.

We can all tell stories about things that have happened to us in threes. It stands to reason that we should follow up in threes.

- Call your potential client three days after you met them.
- If they don't call you back, call them again three days later.
- Now if they don't call you back, wait three weeks and call them again.

If they still don't call you back, leave it alone. They may have gotten busy and want to call you back, but it is not a priority for them. You may run into them at another event and they will most likely say to you, "Sorry I owe you a phone call, but I've been dealing with XYZ issue. Let's schedule a time for us to continue our conversation." If you had kept calling them every day, they may have let you drop off your proposal and then thrown it in the garbage. They may even have just met with you the one time to get you to stop harassing them, and then the proposal still ends up in the garbage. You will never know if you could have gotten the client, because you blew the opportunity by bugging them.

A good time to call a prospective client is before 9 a.m. or after 5 p.m., as they are more likely to answer their own phone at that time. Usually the assistant or secretary will answer during normal business hours to take a message, and rarely will they put you through. They are called the gatekeeper for a reason. Calling on a Monday or Friday is a bad idea. On Monday, they are catching up on any issues that have arisen over the weekend. On Friday they are trying to clear out their "IN" box so they can perhaps duck out early for the weekend. This is especially true on a holiday weekend. Plan to make your calls early or late on a Tuesday, Wednesday, or Thursday.

How Often Do You Network?

I frequently get asked, "How often should I network?" Three times a week is a good number, (again the three rule). What counts as networking?

- Attending a group event
- Having coffee with a new contact
- Meeting with a current client

Any time you are talking about your business or getting to know someone else's business, counts toward your three opportunities. You have to remain open to talk to people about your business. If you are nervous, here are some additional tips to help get you started networking:

- Practice talking to people at non-business events e.g. kids soccer games, grocery store
- Find common ground to start a conversation. If you are at the same event, ask how they are involved in XYZ or how they know the hostess
- Compliment them on something they are wearing and ask where they go it

Talking to Strangers

You may be saving to yourself, "This is all great, but the thought of talking to strangers scares me. I freeze up." I have the solution for you. Practice in a non-threatening environment. Talk to people at the grocery store, at your child's soccer game, anywhere that there are people. Don't worry about discussing business when you practice. You can talk about the groceries the person in front of you is buying. Pick an item that looks interesting to you and ask them a question about it. If you are at a soccer game, ask the parents next to you which one is their child. Comment on how difficult it is to rush from work to make it to the game. Bring up something that interests you or ask for some advice. You don't have to bring up your business. Remember you are just getting comfortable talking to strangers. Once you have done this a few times it does get easier. If they ask what you do, feel free to tell them. I was in traffic court, yes, for the dreaded speeding ticket, and I started chatting with the woman next to me (it seemed like it took forever to see the Judge). We were chatting away about our offenses and she asks me what I did besides speeding. I jokingly told her that I have to speed from one client to the next, because my customers want service now. I told her that I own a janitorial business and she became excited. You would have thought I told her that she won the lottery. In a way she did. As it turns out, her husband was looking for a cleaning company and was having very little luck. A simple, "How do you do?" turned into a contract. While this scenario may not always happen, you will steadily get more comfortable talking to people.

If you are the type of person who never knows what to say to start the conversation, I have two options for you and it really depends if you are talking to a man or woman.

When speaking to a woman you can compliment her on something she is wearing. Perhaps she has on a very colorful scarf. You may say to her, "What a great scarf. Where did you get it?" Women love to talk about their stuff.

When talking to a man, you want to get right to the point. You may say, "What type of business are you looking to get in front of?"

Once the conversation gets going, make sure you are asking open ended questions. You don't want to ask all yes or no response questions. These will only stop the conversation and lead to awkward silences. Some examples of questions you can ask are:

- What is an ideal client for you?
- Is there someone here that you would like to meet?
- How did you get started in your field?
- What products or services do you offer?

We have talked about how to dress, how to start the conversation and even how to follow-up. The most important question is where do you network?

Where to Network

If you are unsure of what groups are out there you can Google networking and see what comes up in your area. Ask your colleagues where they go. Most communities have a Chamber of Commerce and Toastmasters groups. Ideally, you can network anywhere that there is a group of people; a cocktail party, opening night at the opera, etc. There doesn't need to be a huge number of people to make it a successful networking event. I often prefer a smaller number. There may be a hundred people there, but how many will you actually be able to talk to and follow up with? You often feel pressure to talk to them all. This is almost impossible as you would have time to talk to each person for about three seconds. How can you possibly make a good impression in that time while running around the room handing out your business cards?

When you take your time, breathe normally and smile, people will be drawn to you. It is better to meet three good people who you can follow up with, than to grab cards from 20 people who you have no real idea what they do. Remember: you still need to follow up with these people using the "Three Rule."

The point is to get out there and talk about your business!

3
Goals

You have been networking. Business is starting to come in. The problem is how do you know if you are on the right track?

Setting your goals can be very rewarding and I mean that literally (we will discuss rewards later in the chapter). When you first start out, you need to know how much business you would like coming in every week, month, and year to keep your company running successfully financially. That means how much money needs to come in to pay the bills *and* have extra money to pay yourself, *and* reinvest in the company?

Setting Goals

It is much easier to work towards a number than to just go out there and hope for the best. If you are only one sale away from your goal, you are more likely to push through the no's and close the final deal. Setting your goals will be what helps motivate you when things get tough. When your business is running smoothly, life is easy, but it will not always be that way. You need something to push you when the business falls on hard times. The first three years can be the worst. If you can get past this part, it usually gets better. People will often blame the economy, and while this does play a small part, it is not the only factor. You need to convince the potential client that they cannot live without your service. You need to get in front of them in order to do this. Setting your goals can help.

When I first started my business I met the most phenomenal woman named Gail Kendig (P.I.N.K. Inc. **P**owerfully **I**nfluencing Using **N**uggets of **K**nowledge). She talked to me about goals and how to achieve them. Gail started the conversation with "Face it, we hear about goals all the time, but how important it is to reach your goals? You should write them down, even tell someone your plans to achieve your goal(s). How many people do you know that actually do turnkey Goal Setting?"

She elaborated by saying, "As a coach for close to 200 clients (I coached in pairs), I quickly realized that even though these people were paying my company thousands of dollars a year for coaching, many of them were not doing the work. Realizing early on that most of them were stuck, I had to figure out what was happening. Yes, there is something to be said for the value of a product, and if they were paying a hefty price it would have more value to the client. That being said, it didn't! They still didn't do the work. A handful of these clients were seeing success, and that was a small hand. Again, I just had to figure out, why?"

Gail added that as she did her research it came down to our daily living, daily rituals, basically our habits. Gail shared, "Let me tell you habits are very, very difficult to break. Here's the good news. Habits can be broken. The question is, how bad do you want what you don't have and how bad do you want to become unstuck? You have to answer that question first before you can go forward. Make a decision and rearrange your daily living schedule and create new rituals or routines. You must replace the bad habits that are not serving you and create the ones that will align with your ultimate goal."

I went home and told my husband, "Gail says we need to set goals." He looked at me like I was nuts. His response was, "Who is this Gail woman?" After a lot of debating and arguing we sat down and wrote out our goals. At the end of the year we had reached our goals and even surpassed them. Needless to say the next year my husband said to me, "Gail says we have to set our goals. So what are we going to shoot for?" I didn't know what to say. Originally he was skeptical of this idea and now he was pushing for it. My thought from that day on was, try it, if it doesn't work, just don't do it again.

Define Your Goal

The first step to setting your goals is defining what you want to achieve. Be as specific as possible. Don't just say "I would like to sell around $50,000 to $100,000." Which one is it? Do you want the goal to be $50,000 or $100,000? Remember, you want to be realistic. Don't set it so high that you can't achieve it or so low that you reach it within a week. No one says I am going to lose 50 pounds in a week. If someone knows of a diet where this happens, please let me know! You would be making a lot of women happy.

Once you have the magical number in your head, write it down. Next, break the number down into mini-goals. Let's take the $100,000 example. If I set a mini-goal of $10,000 a month in sales I would have 10 months to reach my goal.

That would give me two additional months if I had a slow month. $10,000 seems like a much more manageable number than $100,000. I would write the month January and $10,000 next to it and so on. The best part of writing things down is the satisfaction of crossing it off when you have accomplished your goal. Be sure

~~January $10,000~~
~~February $10,000~~
~~March $10,000~~
April $10,000
May $10,000
June $10,000
July $10,000
August $10,000
September $10,000
October $10,000

and place your written goals where you can see them on a daily basis.

Goal Achieved by Heather Smith

My friend Heather Smith tells a great story about what happened to her when she wrote her goals down.

Stephen R. Covey tells us to "begin with the end in mind" in his book 7 Habits of Highly Effective People. I think this concept is essential. You must first have goals in mind and you must, must, must write them down! The more specific in nature your goal is, the more likely you are to achieve it. Remember that your mind will only accomplish as much as you tell it to, and it will never achieve what is truly possible until you tell it to. My suggestion is take a day to go somewhere serene where you can clear your mind of all the "white noise" that runs through it during your daily activities. Once you get to the park, or the library, or your yard, or wherever you feel completely relaxed wait 30 minutes before you think about anything. After you feel relaxed start to visualize who you want to be, where you want to be, what you want to have, or what you want for your life. Start to write these things down. Make sure you have short and long term goals, but be careful to only write the things that you truly want to accomplish and are most passionate about. Keep it simple and record no more than six to seven goals. Prioritize them in order of importance to you and be as specific as possible. Set deadlines and timelines for your goals. If you have a goal sitting out there without an end date, how does your mind know when it has to complete it? After you have gone through this exercise display your goals boldly wherever you can see and focus them on them daily. It is truly amazing how visual we are, and how we will make sure we accomplish what we believe we can. This practice may seem elementary to you, and it is, and it works! I would like to share with you a recent story from my own life.

I spent a Thursday afternoon out of the office, away from all of my employees, coworkers, family, everyone. I was completely alone to rest my mind and put myself at peace so that I could just think; think about what is really important and what my defined goals truly are. I must share with you that I am not a long term planner. I think the five-year plan makes almost no sense. If I looked at my life five years ago, I couldn't possibly have created goals that made any sense for my life now, as things have changed drastically in five years. Not just with your life, but with technology, world events, and with people that are in your life. In any event, I thought about what I really was passionate about; what was truly in my heart and soul. I came up with a list of six things. I would share each one but only one of them is significant for this story right now. Listed on my yellow pad was Get to Alaska, Tanzania, and Australia. There are a few things that are a little odd about this, including the fact that I wrote "Tanzania." I have had the same three places to go on my bucket list for the last 20 years and I usually refer to these places as my three "A's" Alaska, Africa, and Australia. Today, for some unconscious reason, I wrote Tanzania specifically, which is specifically where I want to go in Africa. So I feel very good about my writing and decide I will put them on my wall at work tomorrow when I can type them clearly (if you saw my writing you would understand).

Later that day, about five hours later to be exact, I am meeting my friend for dinner and yoga, which we try to do periodically. When she sits down we catch up and talk about the latest in each other's lives and she shares with me that she is a little bummed. My friend who has been going through messy divorce proceedings for the past two years had planned a phenomenal trip with her friend, but just this week that friend called to say she had to back out as she just discovered she is pregnant. So I asked, "Where were you going?" Well you may be guessing it by now. She replied "Tanzania and Kenya on safari." "Hmmmm really?" I said, "Well what would you think about me going with you? I would just have to check with a few folks, my husband, my sister (in case I need care for my four- year-old), and my boss." She was a little in shock, because as you can imagine it's not every day when someone who had not planned a trip can just make arrangements on such short notice and go. By the way the trip was now two months out and you have to have reservations, vaccinations, visa etc. I went home to speak with my husband and got the response only the greatest husband in the world would give "Honey, this is a once in a lifetime opportunity, you may never be able to go again; Go for it!" I then called my sister and asked if I needed her could she help with my daughter. She said "Absolutely, you deserve this trip, have a great time!" Last, my boss which I was most unsure about because just a week prior he had told us of a management meeting that he had scheduled in NYC for us during that exact same time. I figured, well I will ask how critical that meeting is and tell him what opportunity has come up. His response? "There will always be other meetings, you deserve this, go and have fun and we will shepherd the herd." Okay, so WOW I am really going to Africa! Do you think this could or would have happened had I not written it down five hours prior? I don't know, maybe it would have, but I do not believe it was pure coincidence.

Lastly I will share that your attitude and outlook affect everything. I expect positive things to happen in my life and they do. I also don't mind taking risks because I always think "what's the worst that can happen if I take this risk?" My answer, is always start all over with just my husband and my daughter, I can do that! I have built everything I am and have to date, I could do it again!

Believe in yourself and your goals, and you will prosper!

Heather A. Smith, LUTCF, CLTC
Financial Architects/MassMutual
heathersmith@finsvcs.com
www.financialarchitectsupstate.com

Reward Yourself

Rewarding yourself is the next step. This is where so many people say, "I can't give myself a present." "Why can't you?" is my response to people. Why are we so caught up in having other people tell us that we did a good job? Why can't we say to ourselves, "I did a good job so I deserve this reward and I am not going to feel guilty about it? I am so worth it!" In order to start, you want to pick mini-rewards. These are small things that you can give to yourself. A few good examples would be a pedicure, a pair of earrings, or a round of golf. Keep the items under $50. Your mini-reward is what is going to keep you going when things are getting tough. You don't want it to be better than the big reward. You get your big reward when you reach the $100,000 mark. I told my husband that when I finished this book I wanted a diamond tennis bracelet, and for each chapter I finish I wanted a new pair of shoes. He is so used to my reward system and how well it works that all he said was, "No problem dear, let me know when you need the money."

You can purchase your reward and put it in your office as a motivator to get out there and achieve your goals. If you have to look at your reward every day, you may be a little more eager to work. Remember you can't have it or use it until you reach the goal. I like to cut out pictures of my rewards and put them all over my office, car, and house so that every time I see the picture I get motivated to sell or write. I am afraid if I have the reward too readily available I will just take it, before I reach my goal. I am not a very patient person.

Visualization

There has been a lot of talk over the years about the power of visualization. While it is true that if you can visualize yourself selling $10,000 then it will happen, you still have to do a bit more than just visualize. You have to work toward it! Something I've kept for some time is a dream book. This is a small photo album that I put pictures of things I want in the future. In my dream book I have a picture of books and of a woman in a bikini. These pictures help me to visualize two things that I want: to write a book and to look good in a bathing suit. I can sit there and visualize the way I want to look in a bikini, but if I keep eating those yummy potato chips then all the thinking and visualizing in the world isn't going to help me to achieve my goal. You have to believe that the goal you set can be achieved. If you don't believe in yourself, who will? When I applied for the Rochester Business Ethics Award, I could visualize myself up on stage accepting my award. I had no doubt in my mind that my company was going to win. I had no idea how I was going to do this; I just knew I was going to win. People often give up too quickly; I was only a finalist my first year, but I was not going to let that stop me. I added more information to my application and turned it in again the following year. I not only won the Rochester Business Ethics Award, I went on to win the (National) American Ethics award. What would have happened if I had given up after the first year? I would have lost out on many great opportunities and priceless recognition for my company.

Besides visualizing your goals, you also need to create a plan and decide what steps you need to take to get me to your goal. This is where you really put your feet to the ground and start walking, and I mean that literally. I would literally have to start walking or doing some form of exercise to squeeze into that bikini. What work do you have to do to reach your goals? Write down your answer if you think it will hold you more accountable. Some people just need to make lists.

Take Action

After you develop your plan of attack, you have one more step. This is usually where most people fail. You need to take action. Sounds simple, right? Wrong! Most people just sit around wishing they could have more. Think back on your life and how many times can you remember wanting something and not getting it. Why didn't you get it? Be honest with yourself. The answer may be that you thought it unattainable so why should you try. A lot of people have this mentality and unfortunately it starts at a very early age. Each year thousands of dollars in scholarship money goes unclaimed. Why? Because high school kids feel they aren't qualified enough, someone else will probably get it, so why bother. This happens with grants from the government and even awards. These awards have the potential to get your business free publicity (we will talk about awards later in the book). People are all too often their own worst enemy. I firmly believe there are no mistakes in life, just opportunities missed.

Here are the steps for setting and reaching your goals:

1. Define your goal
2. Write your goal down
3. Break your goal down to more manageable goals (mini goals)
4. Pick out a reward for yourself
5. Visualize yourself achieving your goal
6. Create your plan: how are you going to achieve your goals? i.e.: are you going to cold call, network, or hire a sales person?
7. Take action

Affirmations

This section is for anyone who may be are thinking, "I don't have the confidence to get things done. I get excited as I am reading this book but I just can't do it." I have the solution for you. Create a positive affirmation. This is just a few lines you say to yourself over and over again. It may help to say these lines in front of the mirror. Keep it positive and make sure it reflects what you want to accomplish. For example I may say, "I am a wonderful sales person."

Be positive; your subconscious mind cannot process negatives. Going back to the weight loss example, if you said *I am not fat*, your mind processes this as *I am fat*; your subconscious ignores the "*not*" part. It would be better to say, "I am slender and look sexy in my new bikini." Continually say your affirmation. Affirmations need to be said several times a day. Repetition is the key. Keep saying them until it becomes a reality. I know you feel silly talking to yourself, but have I let you down yet? You can write your affirmation down and read it or you can memorize it. Each person is different. You need to do what is comfortable for you. I like to say my affirmations in front of a mirror. I say them with energy. Don't just say them in a monotone voice. Put some conviction in them. Stare into your own eyes and be proud of what you are saying.

A few examples of affirmations are:

- I prosper at everything I do and I know I deserve good things
- I am my own unique, wonderful, beautiful self
- I am a whiz at sales and enjoy what I do

Before you continue to read on, take a moment to create your affirmation. Don't put it off. Something will come up and you will forget. You are worth it; take the time now to reaffirm how important you are. By waiting you only hurt yourself. Ready, set, go!

4
Branding

According to the American Marketing Association (AMA), a brand is the "Name, term, sign or design, or a combination of them intended to identify the goods and services of one seller or group of sellers and to differentiate them from those of other sellers." That's a mouthful! Basically, a "brand" is what your company stands for. What you have to offer consumers. Branding is not about getting consumers to choose you over the next guy. You want your brand to deliver your message clearly, confirm that you are credible, connect with your potential clients on an emotional level, motivate them to buy, and finally, to create loyalty. If I were to say to you, "Have it your way" you would think of Burger King⸳. A few years ago I could say to you "Where's the beef?" Instantly you would think of a little old lady and Wendy's⸳. Both these companies used these slogans to help brand themselves. They wanted people to hear or see certain things and instantly think of their business. If I showed you a picture of the McDonalds and Nike logo, you would instantly know who I was talking about. These companies have achieved brand recognition.

What Goes Into a Brand?

To have a successful brand you have to understand the wants and needs of your clients. This is not set in stone. Just as your company grows and changes, your clients' needs and wants will change as well. It's your job to keep up with them.

When branding your company, keep your message consistent. This means that your logo should be the same on your letterhead, business cards, and name tags. If you have a catch phrase, put it on your brochures, website, and any printed material. This will help your clients better understand and recognize your business at a glance.

My good friend Jerry of Schoen Place Auto has a few great ideas about branding that I want to share with you.

Branding Yourself by Jerry Elman

There are all kinds of books, experts and things written about branding yourself. However, this is an extremely complex issue and those who claim to be experts can only offer things to think about and work through in finding the right branding approach. In the end the answers come from within.

Most branding approaches unfortunately miss the mark. I went through over two years of mistakes before I finally figured it out. Branding is not about "buzz words," gimmicks or catching people's attention. Branding is about defining you and your business and then delivering. It's about defining the things that are important in best exceeding the needs and expectations of customers. Branding is different from business to business. That's why the books and experts cannot offer the answers.

If anyone goes into business "just to be like everyone else" in that same business, they are doomed. Everyone else is already doing that! One more business doing that is not going to get customers and take business away from the others!

Before I decided to buy my auto business, I thought long and hard about what I wanted to accomplish and what would make my business different than others in the car business. I have friends that tried once to be in the restaurant business. They failed and had to close after two years of losses. They never got the volume they needed and never developed a loyal following. Their food, service, and environment were actually quite good. So why did they fail? It's simple actually. They built the business around themselves and their personal likes and dislikes. They made every decision down to the menu on what they personally preferred to eat. They never thought about the business as needing to reach out to the tastes and desires of a customer base. They spent a ton of money thinking that if they just offered an environment and menu they personally loved, the place would be packed. The irony is that they offered good fresh food and a nice environment. It just was not an environment and menu that very many people wanted. They treated their restaurant the same as how they would have served friends at their own home, only now they wanted to do this as a business. Needless to say, the business failed and they were angry and bitter that customers would not support them.

In my own experience, I listed all the positives and negatives of how auto businesses met the needs and expectations of customers. I asked friends and people I knew what their likes and dislikes were about being a consumer with auto businesses. What I learned in the end was that it was not about cars and car repairs by themselves. It was about the experience, hassles, and fears most people have when buying or repairing a car. People feel that:

- They are being taken advantage of and ripped off;
- It's a hassle to deal with car businesses;
- Car businesses are all about profit and greed and not about meeting customer needs.

My conclusion was that the product of being in the car business is selling and repairing cars. To me that has to be what I call "table stakes."

The table stakes I defined were: selling reliable, high-quality cars; providing honest, fair prices; and performing car repairs right the first time. To me everyone in the car business should be delivering these basic table stakes. The sad thing is that most are not. So my branding started with these table stakes. We would only sell high quality cars, provide honest, fair prices, and perform car repairs right the first time. But that had to be the basic starting point. What would really make the difference in the eyes of customers would be the *experience* of buying or repairing a car. It had to start with a high standard of ethics and honesty. My goal was to transform this business into the most trusted and respected auto business in the Rochester area, if not beyond.

I then expanded into relationship building. I wanted to eliminate the fear and hassle people faced when dealing with their cars. The more I thought about it, the more the doctor-patient relationship came to mind. The doctor-patient relationship is generally one based on trust, openness, a high degree of competence, being there for the long haul, and developing a long term relationship where each patient's history and needs are known at all times. You do not start the relationship and history from scratch each time that you visit your physician. I was determined to build a business model and culture where both the customer and their car would be known to us like a physician knows their patients. I put together a list of all the hassles and inconveniences people face in buying or repairing a car. I then developed solutions we would offer to those hassles and inconveniences. We would offer free loaner cars, rides to and from work to take the hassle out of getting the car to us and then getting to work or back home. We would offer a clean comfortable waiting room and restroom to customers, and high-quality free refreshments to help them feel at home while they waited for repair work to be performed. I was determined to create a stress-free environment for our customers. We switched to one price "no-haggle" pricing in selling cars. We offer a three-day, 500-mile no questions asked return policy for cars sold. We do not pressure customers into repairs; our focus is on education so that customers can make the decisions best for them when it comes to car repairs. We act as consultants in helping customers make decisions.

Perhaps the most important area of focus I developed was to do something about the customers who tended to be the most disadvantaged, taken advantage of, and had the worst experiences in dealing with car buying and repairs. Women and seniors fall into this category. Many in the car business brag about how they take advantage of women and seniors as "easy prey." Becoming female- and senior-friendly became the most important part of our business model strategy and branding. I quickly realized getting the trust and business of women and seniors was not easy and was not something you could just declare. While we advertised and tried to get the word out that we were women and senior friendly, the message was self-proclaimed and not viewed as believable or credible. I concluded that I needed credentials that would verify that our claims were true. I pursued and obtained formal female-friendly business certifications from two nationally recognized female consumer advocate organizations. Since such certifications do not exist for seniors, I linked with many senior advocates organizations and assisted living facilities to become known and recognized by them. Those organizations now help get the word out to seniors for us. I also became personally involved in organizations focused on women and seniors. Being personally engaged and involved because I truly care has become an important part of my brand.

The last, but perhaps most important lesson I learned in branding is that the people employed with you can make or break any strategies and branding plans that you put in place. As time went on I came to realize the biggest barriers to my plans and direction were the people I employed. This is especially true when you buy an existing business and start making changes. As much as I tried to coach, train, explain, and change the thinking and behaviors of my employees, I found that they were determined to fight me to keep things the way that they wanted, and were too well ingrained in the bad practices that I was determined to change. They thought we should still be "just like" every other car business. I realized I would fail without a team that believed in me and was committed to the same ethics, beliefs, and objectives that I had. One by one I ended up replacing the entire staff. Even then, I made hiring mistakes and replaced people with the wrong people. It took two and a half years to finally put the entire team in place that provides the culture, beliefs, and behaviors that fit with how I want to do business. Once I had the right team in place, not only did my personal stress level drop, but the business started growing and the word about us started getting out faster. I attribute my dedicated and committed employees to this growth.

In summarizing, the key purpose and approaches to branding are:

1. **Define your own "personal competitive advantage":** What are you personally bringing to the table that differentiates you from all the others? If you cannot define your personal competitive advantage, you probably should not even go into business.

2. **Define the competitive advantage of your business:** What can your business bring to the table in making the customer experience and value much more positive and different than current providers? What difference do you want to make in

going into business? What game changers can you provide in ethics and honesty, relationship building, customer conveniences, etc. that the others don't provide? It's got to be much more than just selling the product or service you offer. You have hundreds, if not thousands of competitors already offering those very same products or services. And if people are happy with them or don't believe anyone else is better, they are not going to switch to someone else. What can you offer that the others don't, that customers will recognize, appreciate, and switch their business to you for?

3. **Identify and establish game changers:** What game changers can you bring to the table that totally change the playing field to your advantage in offering the product and service you sell? Game changers are things so different that your competitor's initial reaction is that you are "nuts" and to not even take the threat present to them seriously.

4. **Find the right people:** Having the right employees who are committed to and deliver what you promise will make or break your success. Ultimately how employees act and behave becomes your "brand" in the eyes and ears of customers. They make your branding a reality or a lie.

5. **Build trust:** No one is perfect and certainly no one in business can perform 100% each and every time with a customer. Perhaps the ultimate test of branding is how you come across and deliver when there is a problem or a customer expectation is not met. The true test of a brand is how the business delivers and performs during a problem. Going above and beyond to make the situation right for a customer creates the ultimate trust and belief in a brand. Never, ever let a problem or unhappy customer go away without doing all you can to sincerely and fairly resolve the situation and show that you

truly care and stand by what your branding promises. This is an area many businesses overlook and never figure out. It's like true friendships. We learn who our true friends are, not during good times, but in bad times. Our true friends are always there for us in bad times. Same thing applies in business. In my business we don't always repair cars right the first time, but when we don't we do everything possible to make it right for the customer. I've found that enhances the trust and credibility we have with our customers.

Jerry Elman
Schoen Place Auto
www.schoenplaceauto.com
(585) 381-1970

Employee Uniforms

Let's take a moment to talk about employee uniforms. Your employees are usually the first person/interaction that clients will have with your company. What image are your employee's portraying of your company? If I said to you brown shorts and brown shirt, who would you think of? Yes, UPS. Most people know UPS drivers on site by their uniform. Wouldn't this recognition be great for your company? Well uniforms can help. Uniforms keep your employees looking nice and consistent without having to worry about someone dressing inappropriately. One of my employees came to work in a half shirt, not something I wanted to see. Another one used to come in with low cut shirts. This is not how I wanted my company portrayed. By giving them shirts, I can now have them all looking the same, and no one can argue that I am being unfair.

Name tags should have your company logo on them as well. This will help your clients to know the first names of your employees so that they will be able to bond with each other. The sale then becomes a bit more personal. Business is personal; people like to do business with their friends. Your employees may not become friends with your clients, but your clients may at least feel as if they know them a bit better. At Christmas time each year, a few of my clients leave the cleaners in their buildings a Christmas card and a small gift for each of them, with their names on it.

Brochures

Your brochure is essentially a shortened version of your website. Just as your infomercial is a way to entice a potential client into a follow-up meeting, your brochure becomes your backup. This is what your prospect will take back to their office to share with the rest of their team. With brochure in hand, they can relax and listen to what you have to say. They are not forced to try and remember every fact you may give them. There is a game that is played at baby showers where items are put on a plate and you have 30 seconds to memorize as many items as possible. The plate is then taken away and you have to repeat all of the items that you remember. I have yet to meet the person who can memorize them all. This is not what I want potential clients to do. You can help your employees to feel important by asking them to help design the brochure, and perhaps to be in some photos. This is a double win for you. You get some free marketing help, and employees who feel their opinions count, tend to care a bit more about the company they are working for. This in turn means that they will work a bit harder for you.

Website

Now comes the exciting part, your website. There used to be a saying, "If you are not in the phone book, you are not a legitimate company." How times have changed. The saying now goes, "If you don't have a website, you don't exist." Things that are in print are almost outdated before they can even be printed. By contrast, you can post information online, and in a matter of seconds, have thousands of people reading it. To print this information up on a flyer and distribute it to that many people would cost you a fortune. We have become a society of bloggers, Googlers, and web surfers. I tried to explain to my husband (he's a little computer challenged) that this new generation does not call up their friend and ask for a referral to a business they may need. No this generation, will look for blogs about it, see how many stars it was rated, or what was tweeted about it. A web presence is a must have if you want to survive in this new business world.

Now don't panic if you are not a computer programmer. You can hire someone to design a website for you, or you can purchase a template of one and create it yourself. I recommend you hire someone. They will be able to customize exactly what you want. A website can cost you anywhere from a few hundred dollars to several thousand. You have to decide how much information you want on your website. If money is tight, you can always start out with one page, and later add more pages. This will allow clients to do a web search on you. This is also a good way to design your site. It's best to not look at the whole website in one sitting, break it down to a page at a time. You will probably never be able to say, "my website is complete." I keep finding new things to add to mine all the time. You want to give people a reason to keep going back to your website as well. Perhaps you offer them a free report if they give you their contact information. You can also have them sign up for a newsletter that you send out on a regular basis. The big question then becomes, what goes into your website? First you want to make sure it is easy to navigate, to move around. If people have to go digging to find out who you are and what services you offer, they will most likely look elsewhere. You can have pages such as:

About Us

Awards

Clients

Services

In the News/Press Releases

Community Involvement

Newsletter Archive

I could go on and on, but I think you get the point. Your website has endless possibilities, and if done right can bring you endless clients.

Online Presence by Emily Carpenter

Your company website is a great start to your online presence, but it is only the beginning. When is the last time you Googled your company name, or your own name for that matter? What comes up? Chances are that even if you have not personally put anything up on the web yourself, your name and company name are already there. If I search on my name, I can see a list of every town I've ever lived in, how old I am, and the names of my relatives. If I search on my company name, I can find pages upon pages of links to places that my company name appears. The best way to be sure that your company name comes up high in search engine results is to build a formidable online presence that leads back to your primary website.

Social media is an excellent tool for growing an online presence. There are hundreds of social media sites, but a few stand out from the rest:

- **Facebook:** Connect with friends with a personal profile, and connect with customers with an official business page and Facebook ads. Run Facebook promotions where customers have to Like your page in order to be eligible to win prizes. Create applications (apps) to further enhance customer experience.

- **YouTube:** Demo products and services and launch creative advertising and promotions. Ask customers to give a short testimonial that you can capture on video with a pocket video camera.

- **Twitter:** Reach your customers with short 140-character messages. Include announcements of job openings, new blog posts, and special promotions.

- **LinkedIn:** Create a company profile, groups, post jobs, advertise, and find new employees.

Social media is all about conversation. While true that it allows you to communicate with customers, it also allows customers to communicate with you. Take the opportunity to connect with customers and find out their likes and dislikes based on what they're saying. You will lose people's interest if all you talk about is how great your company is. Consider what your customers are interested in, and find ways to engage them on that level, such as links to informative articles or interesting facts.

Since you can't possibly be active in every social media site, it's important to find a way to monitor what people are saying about your company. Google Alerts (http://www.google.com/alerts) is a free way to be alerted any time someone mentions keywords online that you specify, such as your company name. For instance, if a customer has a bad experience with your restaurant, and tweets about it on Twitter, you will receive a Google alert. This alert gives you a chance to quickly respond to your customer, and has the potential of turning them around to liking your restaurant again. Respond to the nice comments as well with a thank you.

Google also provides free website statistics with Google Analytics (http://www.google.com/analytics/). Once you embed a small amount of code into your website, you can see what pages of your website are the most popular, how visitors are finding you (referring sites), what they're clicking on, how long they stay on any given page, and what part of the world they are from. You can extend the power of Google Analytics with apps available in the Google Analytics Application Gallery (http://www.google.com/analytics/apps/). Having this information available will help you to decide what strategies work on your website, and where you can make changes to improve overall site performance. Most website hosts also have options for analytics available through your site's control panel. If you're not familiar with what your web host offers, click around or give them a call.

Larger companies may need a paid social media monitoring service such as Radian6 (http://www.radian6.com/) or SM2 (http://socialmedia.alterian.com/) to collect and analyze data. These services can even alert you to the tone of someone's post, such as sarcasm or anger so that you can respond appropriately.

A blog is another important aspect of your online presence. A blog is simply a space to educate your customers with short "articles" that provide valuable information in your field. For instance, a heating and cooling company may have a blog about energy efficiency and indoor air quality. Potential customers interested in those topics will do a Google search and find their blog, which in turn could lead to a sale. Search engines such as Google, Yahoo, or Bing, love blogs because of their vast amount of information and frequent updates.

A blog contains much of the same information that is traditionally found in a company newsletter. If you are already creating a newsletter, then you already have the process in place to create articles that could be posted to your blog. The difference is that a paper newsletter reaches a limited number of people that may or may not read it, and is thrown in the recycling bin, never to be read again. A blog, however, is searchable by the world and remains available indefinitely.

A blog can be simple to start with online services such as Blogger (http://www.blogger.com) or WordPress (http://www.wordpress.com). WordPress is also available as a download that you can install on your web host (http://www.wordpress.org). If you choose to install WordPress on your own server, it is a good idea to choose a web host that offers tools to install WordPress with a touch of a button. If your host doesn't provide such a tool, you can use SimpleScripts (http://www.simplescripts.com/) for free to do the installation for you. By installing it yourself, you can host WordPress blogs on multiple domains for the one price of your annual web hosting fees. No additional fees are due to WordPress.

An e-newsletter is another effective way to send updates to interested customers. An e-newsletter can be a simple as a summary of the latest articles on your blog, and perhaps any contests or specials that you are currently running. An e-newsletter should be a teaser to prompt readers to link to your blog or website. Include the start of your prominent articles, with links to see the full article on your blog or website. Using a service such as Constant Contact will help you to manage lists, comply with SPAM laws, and deliver a consistently branded message to your customers.

An often overlooked area of search strategy is location searches. What comes up if you do an address search for your business' location in Google Places (www.google.com/places/) or MapQuest or Yahoo Local (http://local.yahoo.com/)? Is your business listed on the map? Is the information accurate? If information about your business is inaccurate or missing, then as the business owner, you can update the information yourself. If you have a building that customers come to, then you will also want to be found in GPS search results. Go to the websites for popular GPS manufacturers such as TomTom, Magellan, and Garmin and enter information about your business.

Smartphones are a growing area to consider into your online presence. Have you looked at your company website on multiple smartphones to see what it looks like? Many companies are creating mobile versions of their websites to accommodate mobile users. Android, iPhone, and BlackBerry all have extensive application libraries that people use to get news, locate businesses, find discounts, and make online purchases. Create your own company app or utilize existing applications such as coupon apps that will list your currently available discounts.

Your online presence should not stop at the internet. Include your website address and social media icons on everything including:

- Letterhead
- Print ads
- TV ads
- Radio ads
- Email signature
- Business cards
- Everything

Many people feel overwhelmed with the prospect of keeping up with social media, blogs, a newsletter, and a website. If this sounds like you, start with one change at a time to super size your online presence. For instance, you could start with a Facebook page. Once you have mastered that, add a Twitter account, and so on. No matter what you do, remember that consistency is king. When you add something new, don't neglect everything else.

There are some tools available to help you to manage multiple social media sites. With ping.fm, you can write a message once, and broadcast it to dozens of social media sites in an instant. Desktop and smartphone apps, such as TweetDeck, Seesmic, and Digsby, give you single-point access to multiple social media accounts. CoTweet (http://www.cotweet.com) is an excellent tool if you'd like to have multiple team members managing a single Twitter account. Their standard account is free, with an option to upgrade to an enterprise edition.

Online tools and technology are changing every day. The longer you wait to become a part of it, the further behind you'll be when you do start. Get training if you need it, but nothing is a better teacher than experience. Start now!

Emily Carpenter
WhizBang! Web Solutions LLC
www.whizbangweb.com
(585) 288-7254

Your Personal Message as Branding

When I first meet people they ask what I do. I used to tell them that I own a janitorial company. They would instantly ask if I clean houses. I would have to tell them no. By saying no they would shut down and not want to talk to me further. People don't like being told no, for any reason. I had to find a better way to explain what I did. Now when someone asks me what I do, I say, "I am cleaning up Rochester (the town I live in) one office at a time." This statement explains that I clean offices and not houses. The people I meet no longer have to ask for clarification. One statement quickly explains what I do. I encourage you to take a moment and think about what you will say when someone asks you what you do for a living. Keep your statement short. If you can't say it in 10 seconds or less, it's too long. This goes back to when we talked about infomercials. You have a short window to capture the attention of your prospective client.

The way you dress is also part of your personal message. As the CEO of your company, you will have to choose the image that you want to portray. I have never been one to wear three-piece suits. For me this seems a bit stuffy. Now don't get me wrong, I still dress nicely, I wear a nice pair of slacks and great shoes. People will often come up to me just to see what new shoes I have. I portray the image of being a down to earth CEO; I am all about being equal to everyone. This look may not be for everyone, you will have to decide what your image is going to say about you.

Voicemail Message

People tend to forget about how important the company voicemail message is and what overall message is conveyed to potential clients when they call you for the first (or any) time. Are you being consistent with your branding message? Whether you have one employee voicemail or 20 employee voicemails, consistency is the key. To make this easy on your employees, you can create a script for them to follow. Some people like to make their voicemail message a funny one. My good friend Emily Carpenter of WhizBang! Web Solutions says she used to call this one particular company all the time because she wanted to hear a good joke. She started telling her friends to call them up as well. This company was giving people a reason to keep coming back. Another really good idea is to put a message for consumers to listen to while they are on hold. You could take a moment and talk about any specials you have going or about some of your products.

This may be the first contact potential clients have with you. I often hate when I call someone and the message says, "I will be out of the office on Monday, please leave a message" and it's Wednesday. There are a few problems with this message.

1. If it's Wednesday, are they in or not?

2. Did I call the right company?

3. They have missed an opportunity to send me to their website so I can learn more about them.

4. A message that sounded like they were on top of things on Monday, now sounds like they don't pay attention to detail two days later.

They would have been better off saying, "You have reached (insert name) at (insert company name). I have stepped away from my desk, please feel free to leave a message and I will return your call. You can visit our website at (insert web address) to learn more about us. Have a great day!"

Sending people to your website is the easiest way for people to learn more about you. They can browse your site at their leisure. If they have questions, you will be able to answer them when you call them back without having to waste time explaining what you have to offer.

Use your catch phrase at the end of your message to reinforce your branding. If you do this though, people will come to expect it. My friend Gail always says, "Stay beautiful" at the end of her voicemail message. She is known for always being positive, happy, and motivating. I can't remember a time when she might have been sad. One day I called her house and noticed that she had changed her message. It no longer said "Stay Beautiful" at the end. My heart sank. Instantly, I thought she must not be well. I left her a frantic message to call me back ASAP. A little while later she called me and before she could even say hello, I asked her if she was alright. Her reply was, of course, I am fine, why do you ask? I explained to her that she didn't say "stay beautiful" at the end of her message. She started laughing and told me when she recorded her message she was in a hurry and forgot to add it. I had become so used to her saying it that when it wasn't' there, I thought that surely something had to be wrong.

Promotional Products

Another great way to brand your company is to use promotional products. These are the handy giveaways that you find at tradeshows and events. Most companies choose to use pens. This is a great idea. Who hasn't been somewhere and couldn't find a pen? Your company name has the potential to travel very far, and be in many hands. Water bottles are also a good one, especially in the summer when people drink the most water. As a society we have become very green-conscious. What better way to show people your company cares about the environment than with refillable water bottles with your company logo on them? Or those great grocery bags, these help save plastic bags from going into our landfills?

I have always wanted to get some broom key chains to promote my janitorial company. I used to know a chiropractor that had spine key chains. He would hand them out and people would look at him a bit funny, and then they would ask him what they were supposed to be. He would start a conversation with them about how he was a chiropractor, and could help adjust their spine. It was a good ice breaker. The best thing about promotional products is that people pass them on to their friends. These are people who you may have not had the chance to meet otherwise, but that are hearing about your company anyway. Choose an item that best fits with your company and your beliefs.

Brand consistency

One of the things that I always say is that "it starts at the top." Your job as the owner is to set the example, and your employees will follow what you do. Don't send mixed messages. By creating written guidelines, there will be no question as to your company's position or core values. Employees will better understand what your company stands for and will be better able to handle customer issues as well as feedback in a consistent manner.

Branding guidelines should also cover visual consistencies such as colors, logo, fabrics for clothing, font, and anything else that makes your brand unique. Something as basic as defining what font to use in letters can make a big difference in how your brand is perceived by customers.

Brand consistency is paramount and is also what usually unravels first. Many things will come up that need attention in your business. It is important to establish checks and balances for all portions of your business, but especially for your brand. Every employee should be allowed to identify and address any inconsistency with your brand. They are on the frontline interacting with clients, and are in a position to notice inconsistencies first. Empowering them to fix problems is a win-win situation. They will do a better job for you if they feel that they have a say in the company, and your clients will be happy that the issue was resolved quickly.

Customer Service

Branding and customer service go hand in hand. Did you know that depending on your industry, it can cost anywhere from four to seven times more to get a new customer than it would cost to keep a current customer happy? The average business never hears from 96% of its unhappy customers. The following poem sums this up nicely:

Remember Me?
(Author unknown)

I'm the person who asks: "How long is the wait?" You tell
me ten minutes…but it gets very late.
I'm the person who sees:
The whole staff loiters
While my waitress does everything
But take my order.
I'm the person who says:
"That's not what I ordered…but its O.K.
I'll eat it anyway."
I'm the person who calls:
To see if my lost item was found
And all I get is a run-around.
I'm the person who leaves:
With a slight frown
Cause the hostess is nowhere to be found.
I'm the person who should
Write a negative letter
But feel it wouldn't make anything better.
Yes, you might say that I'm a good guy…
That I understand that you kind of try.
But, please read on and you will see…
That there's another side of me.
I'm the person who
Never comes back
Because of something you tend to lack.
It amuses me to see you spending
Thousands of dollars on ads never ending
In an effort to get me back into your place
When you hardly even remember my face.
In order to keep me as a guest
I have but one simple little request…
When I am here all you have to do
Is give me the service I'm entitled to.

It is a pretty powerful message. I encourage everyone to make a copy and give it to all your managers and employees. Of the customers who do complain, between 54% and 70% will do business again with you if their complaint is resolved, and if the customer feels their complaint was resolved quickly the number goes up to 95%.

It will take you 12 positive experiences to make up for that one negative experience. Twelve is a lot of positive customer experiences. What is to say that the customer is going to come back that many times?

My husband and I went to a local chain restaurant. We stood at the podium for 20 minutes while numerous wait staff walked right by us. Now some of you may be thinking that it's not their job to seat us. While this is technically true, I believe it is everyone's job to make the customer feel welcome. If your employees have the mentality that, "It's not my job. I'm not doing that." then it's time you teach your employees that it's everyone's job. If they refuse to comply then you may want to replace them. If you don't agree with me, I suggest you reread the statistics on customer service.

Back to my example, as my husband and I are getting more and more angry at being ignored, two young gentlemen walk in. We turned to them and sarcastically said, "Good luck getting a table." Their response was, "How long have you been waiting?" While I would have loved to have told them, to our amazement the same waitress who walked past us numerous times and ignored us was only too happy to help these two gentlemen. She was young and so were they. We had just been discriminated against because of our age. We couldn't believe it! And to make matters worse, she seated the two guys and ignored us. We grabbed a server and asked to speak to the manager. The manager came out and we explained to him what had just happened. To add insult to an already bad situation, he said to us "She's young. What can you expect?" There was no apology. No, I will seat you myself. There was no, let's try and make this situation better. He then said, "I will get someone to seat you" and walked off. Why couldn't he seat us? We were so mad that we proceeded to walk out. We had reached a point where we felt that nothing could have made the situation better. This happened five years ago. To this day, we have never gone back to that restaurant. Now every time we drive by with anyone else in the car, my husband tells the story of what happened to us.

Don't get me wrong. I am the first person to ask for a manager to compliment someone on good customer service. I am also the one who speaks up when things go wrong. My belief is that if you don't tell them what is wrong or what you don't like, how can they fix it?

This brings me to the six strategies for good customer service:

1. **Demonstrate optimal customer service:** It starts at the top and works its way down (sound familiar, similar principle to branding). As the **owner** or manager you want to show/ explain to your employees the importance of good customer service. If they hear you bad mouthing a client, what do you think they are going to do? If they see you fixing a problem quickly, they are more likely to do the same. You can also go out in the field and ask your clients how their experience was. Is there something you can do to better serve them? Who better to ask what they like or don't like than the client themselves?

2. **Get feedback/make changes:** Asking for feedback is a good start, but let's add another step. Use the feedback and make the necessary changes. If you are unable to speak to clients directly (perhaps they are out of state) send them a survey. When using a survey, you will get a better response if you

offer some type of reward for answering. People love to get free stuff. You may also want to put together a focus group and let them discuss what they like or don't like. Be careful; when people know you are listening, they may feel uncomfortable and not tell the truth. If you want to go with the focus group approach, hire a neutral party to conduct it. Again, make sure that you take the advice given and make the necessary changes. There is nothing worse than giving your opinion and finding the same bad customer service issue happening again.

3. **Get your employees involved:** Ask employees how they feel they can improve the **company**. Put out a suggestion box so that if an employee feels uncomfortable speaking out, they can do so anonymously. Once you have the surveys back, you may want to retrain employees on any issues that arise. Remember, if you don't tell them they are doing something wrong, how can you expect them to fix the problem and do it right?

4. **Create customer-friendly services:** Create an atmosphere where your customer walks away happy and fulfilled. I like to speak with a person who is pleasant and attentive to my needs. Even if they **cannot** help me, I will walk away happy if I feel that they have tried their hardest. Let me give you a very annoying example of customer service. You call up Company X because you have an issue that you would like addressed. You get the lovely automated system that lists all of your options. Every option except for the one you really want, a live person! You go through numerous prompts and after about 20 minutes of your time you might finally get a real live person, only to be immediately asked what your customer ID number is. Now didn't you just punch that

number in a few times? Shouldn't it just come up on their screen? This is so frustrating and not very customer friendly. I always wondered how many people hang up, never get their issue resolved, and never work with that company again.

5. **Develop consistent procedures for everything:** Clients don't like change. They like to call you up and order product X the same way every **time** they call. If they want to return something, they want it to be the same way they returned something two months ago. Your employees will thank you as well. If everything has a procedure, employees will not have to guess at how things are done.

6. **Recognize excellence every chance you get:** When your employees do a good job, tell them. I was in a local grocery store returning some **empty** water bottles. The person behind the counter was so pleasant and helpful; something that in my experience, rarely happens. Most of the time the employees act like they don't want to touch my returnables. I made it a point to ask for the manager. Turns out that if a customer compliments an employee, the employee gets a ten dollar gift card. Who doesn't want an extra bonus? Your employees are the ones who interact the most with your clients. They should be as happy, friendly, and courteous as possible. If you alienate your customers, no matter how much you invest in your brand, your company will not make it. The true test of your brand is your ability to deliver a great customer experience every time.

5
The Secrets to Getting Your Name Out There

When you first start your business you probably won't have a lot of money to spare for advertising. How do you get your name out? Is there some secret? Yes, there are a few simple things you can do.

Be an Expert

Be seen as an expert at something to help get your name out there. Are you passionate about anything? Is there something in particular that you are really good at? Pick an area and brush up on your skills. Do you know enough that you can offer people advice? Start helping others in this field. Word will get out and people will start referring you to others.

The area you choose does not have to be the same field as your business. The fact that you are an expert in anything will get your name out there and have a direct impact on your business. I own a janitorial company, but most people are not interested in hearing lectures about how to best clean their office. I am often referred to as the "networking queen" by my circle of influence. I built my janitorial business by networking. I am often asked for tips on where and how to network. I will meet with people, give them lessons on networking, and discuss my business.

By offering advice to people I am paying it forward. We have all heard the concept of Karma; what comes around goes around. If you do good things, then good things will happen to you. The concept of pay it forward is similar. You do good things for others and at some point in the future, good things will happen to you. By meeting with these people I am able to tell them what I do. They may not know of anyone who has a need for my services then, but perhaps in the future they may meet someone. About four years ago I was at a networking event and I met a lot of people; it was my responsibility to offer networking tips. One of the people called me up four years later to say that the company they were working for was in need of my services. They remembered the advice I had offered them and when the need came up, I was in. By being seen as an expert, people will send others to you. They will want to hear what you have to say. This will help them get to know you better and hopefully buy your services or products.

Become a Speaker

Once you have established yourself as an expert, you can offer seminars on your topic. Seminars can get your company in front of potentially hundreds of people. You would not be able to easily meet that many people individually. Make sure you bring handouts to your presentations that include a summary of your talk and your contact information. People will often take these handouts back to the office and share them with their coworkers, allowing even more people to hear about you.

Most local chambers of commerce and business networking groups are looking for speakers to fill their agendas. If you are nervous about speaking in front of people, try Toastmasters. They will show you techniques for speaking in public and offer feedback and support to help you to improve. You can always start out by reviewing a book on a topic that interests you. This way you won't have to put a whole presentation together. All the material is right there for you. When you do get asked to speak, make sure it will be put in your local newspaper's calendar so that even more people will see your name.

Offer a small raffle item at your event in exchange for people's business cards, such as a business book (you can use this one, I won't mind) or a gift certificate to a local restaurant. Once you have everyone's business cards you can follow up with them later.

Become a Writer

Write articles for your local newspaper or magazine. You may or may not be offered payment for your efforts by the publication itself; however, it is always worth the free publicity you will receive. Hundreds of people will hear about your company. I belong to a local women's group that allows its members to write a column called Women at Work. I have written around seven articles in the past two years resulting in numerous phone calls for potential business. When asked how they heard of us, the reply is, "We saw your article in the paper."

Another way to provide content is to publish your own newsletter or e-zine. Offer advice or tips on your subject of choice in order to build your distribution list. If it's packed full of good information, people will forward it to their friends. Be sure to include your full contact information and give the reader permission to forward or use your article on the condition that they give you full credit. Decide how often you want to send out your newsletter: weekly, monthly or bi-monthly. Stick to your schedule of choice; your readers will come to expect it. A good friend of mine was sending out her newsletter at the beginning of the month like clockwork. Each month I couldn't wait to get it. She would include a great quote, a funny story about her crazy life, and lots of good tips. One month it didn't come. I thought perhaps she was late putting it out. The entire month went by and no newsletter. I had not realized until that moment how much I looked forward to it. I sent her off an email asking if everything was OK. She replied that she has gotten busy with her business and family and there just wasn't time to write it. She went on to say that I wasn't the only one who had noticed. People like things to stay the same. Be consistent.

Send Out Press Releases

Send out a press release whenever something great is happening with your business. Perhaps it is your anniversary or you have reached the million-dollar mark. Newspapers, news channels, and magazines are always looking for stories. A key tip here is that your press release should include how the event affects the community. Reporters want to how your story is helping the community. For example, you just landed a huge new client and will now have to hire X number of employees. Include your contact information at the top and bottom of your press release, making it easy for the reporter to contact you. If you are planning to email your press release, include it in the body of the email rather than as an attachment which is unlikely to be opened by most reporters. When the reporter calls you for a meeting, be willing to rearrange your schedule to make yourself available to them. Reporters often have a short window of time to write a story. You don't want to make it difficult for them. If they like you and find you helpful, they may give your name to other reporters who are in need of a source for a story they are writing. After your story is published, be sure and send a thank you note. You can offer to take them to lunch. This would be a great opportunity to get to know them better and have them get to know you. The better they know you, the easier it is for them to give your name to other reporters, which means your name is in the paper more often.

Become a Sponsor

Sponsoring an event or charity is another way to get your name out there. This one will cost you some money, but is a tax write-off and supports a good cause. Pick something that has meaning to you. One of the common benefits that this type of advertising has to offer is t-shirts. Your company name will be on the backs of a bunch of people. Every time they wear the shirt, more people will see your company name. You may also be listed in the local paper as a sponsor. If there are signs or programs at the event, your name could be listed on them as well. If the opportunity arises to have a tradeshow booth at the event, purchase that too. This table allows you to put samples, information, or those great water bottles out. You won't have to try and carry around all of the information about your company. Booklets may also be available to purchase advertising in. These usually list what the event is about and who is going to be there. People tend to take these back to the office to look through later. They will have all of your information available to them, so that when a need arises, they may remember your ad and call you.

Awards

Applying for awards is a great way to get your name out there and differentiate yourself from the competition at the same time. When you win you may get the chance to give a speech in front of a lot of people. While you have their attention, use it to promote your company. As I mentioned earlier, last year we won the Rochester Business Ethics Award. I knew from attending the previous year, that everyone would be bored by the time it came to announce the winners. I decided to spice it up a bit. I taped a bunch of pieces of paper together to make one long sheet. I wrote a bunch of gibberish on them and rolled them up. When I got up to the podium to give my speech, I started with "Wow, this is like being at the Emmy Awards! There are a few people I'd like to thank after giving my speech." I let the paper unroll and hit the floor. No one spoke; you could hear a pin drop. They were all afraid that I was serious. I waited about three seconds and said, "Just kidding!" They all started laughing. This joke served three purposes: 1) it gave me a moment to collect myself and catch my breath; 2) it ensured that I had everyone's attention; and 3) it got the audience to laugh and relax a bit. Speakers often tell a joke to loosen up the crowd. Make sure your joke is safe and that you won't offend anyone. After I walked off the stage, the medium-size company winner was coming up to give his speech. He stopped me and gave me a hug and said, "Thank you. You loosened them up for me."

Sometimes the winner will get a nice write-up in the paper. If you are really lucky (or the award is prominent enough) the local news channels will be there providing an opportunity for you to get on television.

No matter how you look at it, awards can be very helpful to your business.

6
Sales

Let's face it: sales are personal. There are many different styles and opinions on what works and what doesn't. I decided that with this chapter I am going to have my friends tell their sales stories. As you read through them, look for things that appeal to you. You can model yourself after one person or take parts from different people. As I said, sales are personal and you have to do whatever is comfortable for you.

My Story

What has worked for me is the no-sell approach. Instead of trying to sell my services, I educate people on how my company runs. When I meet a new company who is looking for a bid, I walk through their facility with them as they point out what needs to be done. My partner takes notes as I talk to them about our training philosophy, the awards we have won (remember these awards help you to stand out), and how we treat our employees like family. I tell them about how we handout turkeys for Thanksgiving and give Christmas stockings and birthday presents to show appreciation for our employees. This lets the client know that our services are not the usual run-of-the-mill. Our employees care about their job, which means they will do a better job for the client.

Born to Sell by Terry Glasbergen

Sales: interesting, yet difficult for some. For me, I was born a salesman. My sales career began at age 10 with the 4H Club. We sold light bulbs and cookies, and I sold the most. At age 12 in Boy Scouts I sold the most merchandise in Tom Watt Kits and more light bulbs. While peddling newspapers I doubled my paper route and was nominated paperboy of the year.

Once I realized that my strengths were sales and communications, life was a breeze. Well, maybe more like a lot of wind, but at least I knew what I needed to do in order to succeed. For me it's the hunt, the chase, the dance with my prospects that excites me, and then when I succeed I'm like a kid on Christmas morning. I love to win. I don't win them all, but I do win my share.

Networking

As a sales person you need prospects to talk to, and a lot of them because not everyone in going to buy from you, no matter how good you are. One of my greatest challenges is having enough people to talk to. No matter what I've sold, my challenge was always getting enough prospects to talk to. Then one day it happened: I found the magic bullet. Seriously, there is a magic bullet, not to help me to lose weight, but to meet more people. You might be saying "Sure, a magic bullet. I doubt it!" The magic bullet is called networking. Wow! Up to this point I was in my own vacuum, or the company's vacuum that was created for me by calling the leads given to me, or by just knocking on doors. Although I was a successful salesperson I was also shy, well not shy, maybe just introverted. I knew I needed to meet more people to be more successful, so I began to network with others.

My Raving Fan

What I was really looking for was a Raving Fan. What the heck is a raving fan? Well, it is not your spouse, dog, or kids, but they should be your raving fans too. A raving fan is someone who believes in you, your product or service, and introduces you to others that they feel will benefit from you. Your raving fan will put people in front of you. This person has huge credibility in the marketplace and is connected to hundreds of people.

I went to a networking event and met someone who told me that I must contact K. Well, I called K and scheduled a coffee meeting with me. During our meeting, she rattled off names of people for me to contact. She said to tell them that the crazy redhead K. said that we should talk. I approached several people using K.'s name as my in to meet with them. They instantly agreed to see me! Not just one, but all of them. I was shocked. They saw me because my raving fan had huge credibility. My raving fan put hundreds of dollars in my pocket in a few short months. One day she gave me a box full of business cards of people I should contact using her name. You can't buy that type of a prospecting system anywhere.

My point is to get out of your office or your house or your basement, and get your business in front of people: as many people as possible. People love to help other people. Referral selling is not only a smart way of doing business, it's the best way. If you are not doing it, stop what you are doing and start networking with people.

Having a raving fan is critical to your success and will give you an edge that others may not have. Better yet, become a raving fan for someone. The more you give of yourself the more will come back to you. It's a universal principle and it works.

Engage with your prospect

OK, so I have learned the skill of sales and communication and networking to help me become more successful, but it is how I implement these skills that makes my business successful. So why am I successful? I engage with my prospects. I get to know them to find out what they really need and if I can solve their problem.

That is my real key to success. It's not luck, not skill, not a good prospect list: it is because I like to help people solve their problems. And I do it by asking lots and lots of questions and I do not stop asking questions until I am satisfied that I truly understand their need or problem. Think about it. What if I only asked a couple of questions and jumped into my sales pitch. I may not truly understand the prospects need. So who am I helping really? Me? Because I just want to tell them about this great product that is going to save them time and money? What if he doesn't want to save time and money, but has a totally different need? If you rush into your sales presentation too soon you may lose the sale. This is a rookie mistake, but I see a lot of seasoned sales reps rush into their presentations too. There is no rush. Get to know your prospect, make a new friend. Then tell them about what you have that will help them.

Make a Friend

I try to make my prospect my friend. Not a buddy; a friend. Not a drinking buddy; a friend. Remember, people love to do business with people they like. And people love to talk about themselves. I like to ask questions that get my prospects involved. The more involved they are, the more likely they are to buy from me. When you try this don't be a phony. People can smell when you are being phony from miles away. Take a genuine interest in people. Engage with them. Try it socially at first so that you become comfortable with it. This is a skill that you must learn to be successful with people. People are buying you, regardless of what you are selling. I had a customer with whom I had developed a relationship and over the years my product was a higher price than what he could have bought from one of my competitors. Why? Relationships. As soon as I left the company I was selling for, guess what? My customer switched to another, more inexpensive vendor. If I knew my product was more costly than my competition, I would tell people that not only do you get product X, you get me, and I cost a whole lot more than product X. I have made friends with my prospects all throughout my career. In fact, if I develop a new business or start selling something new, I can always go back to past customers. Maybe comfortably say to them, "Who do you know that does X?" And that is how I get more referrals.

Finally, to excel at sales or anything else, have fun. Keep things light. If you are someone who has a good sense of humor, use it. Humor is a great icebreaker, but you must know when to use it and when to not. If you are not a funny person, don't try to be one. You will come off as phony. Sales work may be difficult and challenging, but make a game out of it and have fun. Most of all; be yourself. Ask questions, find a raving fan, and work your business every day. If you don't, you will be out of business.

Terry Glasbergen
Glasbergen Marketing Services
tglasbergen@gmail.com
(888) 945-7779

Burning Bridges by Kevin Kluth

My friend Kevin has a great take on burning bridges and how this can affect your sales.

Bridges are connectors, enabling you to reach your destination more easily. In the world of business, every person we meet is a "bridge," a connector, to other people that we would like to meet and conduct business with. If you were on a trip, you would never think of destroying a bridge that you had just crossed; you might need to cross that bridge again later! However, we are often tempted to burn bridges in our business dealings with others, the connectors in our lives. *Never* give in to this temptation. These statements may sound very simple; however, they become much harder to live by with the addition of a single element.

Emotion. We must never allow our emotions to get the best of us, no matter how difficult it may seem. No matter if we're already having a bad day. No matter if we feel that we're "in the right," and the other party is the one that's wrong! The value of keeping our emotions in check is illustrated by a true story that recently happened to me in my business. At my business, Pinnacle Cleaning in Rochester, New York, we operate a carpet cleaning service which provides service to residential and commercial clients. One of our major clients is one that we have been servicing for well over ten years, and they report that they have been very happy with our service. One day last year, I received a call from them that went something like this: "Kevin, this is So-and-so from XYZ Co. You've been doing a good job at a fair price, but we'd like to have two contractors to provide service for us. So, I'm informing you that we will still be doing business with you, but we will be giving you half the amount of work we normally do." Wow! It's always nice to receive a call like that, isn't it? How would you have reacted? Before you answer, let me tell you more about the situation: it was around 10:00 am, and I was already having a "bad day." One of our major pieces of equipment broke down, so we were scrambling to provide service to everyone for that day. I'm sure that you can relate to the negative feelings that must have been roiling inside me that morning, "This bad news, on top of an equipment breakdown?" On top of *that*, this call was just two days before we were about to start our busy season with XYZ Co., and I had employees hired and ready to start working. Pardon the pun, but as a carpet cleaning service provider, I felt like the rug had been just pulled out from under me.

I respond by simply saying something like this: "We would be happy to provide you with whatever service you need. I appreciate the work you have given us in the past, and look forward to working with you in the future." That's not to say that it was easy. It was difficult to keep my emotions in check. I looked at my situation the following way: suppose someone gave me a whole blueberry pie as a thank you gift. Great! I love blueberry pie! But, at the last minute, just before I was going to get myself a slice, they took half of it away. How should I feel? Well, isn't fifty percent of a pie better than zero percent of a pie? So, keeping half of a major account was better than losing all of it. That's not to say that I was thrilled with their decision, not by any stretch.

I was determined to not make a bad situation worse by reacting in a harsh manner. Shortly after receiving this phone call, I talked to a few business associates, and I was surprised at how many of them said, "You should have let them know how you feel. You've provided a carpet cleaning service for them for over ten years, and this is how they repay you? I would have quit on the spot! Let them try to find someone as good as you." I have to admit that's how I felt, but I was determined to not show it on the outside.

A good check for your emotions is your company's mission statement. Do you have one for your business? Our mission statement at Pinnacle Cleaning is "To Provide a Totally Outstanding, 'Red Carpet,' Service Experience!" Your mission can serve as a touchstone for everything you do within your business. Let's use my situation as an example. Before reacting emotionally to a negative situation, we can help keep our emotions in check by asking ourselves questions such as, "Is this reaction consistent with our mission statement (to provide outstanding service)?" Is there anything particularly outstanding about reacting harshly to bad news? People do that every day! But, there is something outstanding, or notable, about responding in a positive way. This is especially true when so many others react negatively. Every decision we make is a reflection of our belief in our mission statement. Have we really "bought in" to that statement? Or do we merely give it lip service when convenient? When faced with a decision, small or large, we can choose to move forward by responding in a positive direction. Conversely, we can sidetrack ourselves away from our mission by deciding to react in a negative fashion.

Let's go back to my story. Even if I was informed that I had lost the entire account at XYZ Co., if I had burned my bridges there (reacting negatively), what are the chances that I would ever be asked to service them again? You know the answer to that too; slim to none, right? However, by responding positively, I put myself in line for more possible work in the future. Not only that, but I would have left the chance open for future referrals from this bridge, this connector, that I have left intact. As it stands today, we are still providing service for to XYZ Co. Later the very same day that I received that negative phone call, my contact called me again. Was he calling to give me even more bad news? On the contrary, the second call went something like this: "Kevin, I just got off the phone with your competitor. I made him the same offer I made to you. He reacted by saying, 'If I can't have the whole account, I don't want any of it!' So, what I'm saying is that you still have the whole account. I'm not going to bother looking for anyone else, when you have always provided good service to us." Yes! You can be sure that *that* call made my day. I had plenty of work for my employees, and we had a great year.

However, if I had burned my bridge with that individual, I am certain that he would have looked elsewhere for another carpet cleaning service. Also, consider future possibilities: What if he moved to another place of employment? I would have lost all chances at future work from him at his new location. In addition, what about his entire network? If he was at a party and a friend mentioned that she was selling her house in Rochester, there's no way I would have received a referral to clean her carpeting. Burning that bridge, that connector, for one fleeting moment of self-satisfaction could have cost untold thousands of dollars in future referrals.

Every person you meet, every client you have, is a potential goldmine of future business and referrals. Taking the high road by responding positively, instead of reacting negatively, is always the true professional's wisest course of action. Burning your bridges with a person or company may offer instant gratification, but it always costs in the long run. When the question before you is to burn or not to burn? It is always best answered: DON'T BURN BRIDGES!

Kevin Kluth
Pinnacle Cleaning
www.rochestercarpetcare.com
www.rochesterrugcleaning.com
(585) 309-1990

Value Over Price by Mike Healy

Over the years I have had a few sales positions; I have had some great jobs, and have made OK money. If my price was good, I won the sale...if my price was off, I lost the sale. That is the way it works, right?? If you have the lowest price you win the deal, if you don't have the lowest price you lose the deal. Ahhh, this is typical sales. Four years ago, I had the most interesting opportunity as I interviewed with a Company called Hillyard. Instead of being questioned for an hour, I was told how Hillyard NY operates. I was interviewing with a company that offered many tools that I could combine with my sales skills. Hillyard is a chemical manufacturer and distributor selling gym floor finishes, waxes, cleaning chemicals, and are a jan san (Janitorial Sanitary) company. Why buy from Hillyard? Are we the least expensive? No, and we don't want to be. We offer high quality products at a fair price.

Then why buy from Hillyard? Since Hillyard is not the cheapest out there, the answer boils down to value. We bring value to our customers above and beyond what our competitors offer.

Hillyard taught me a new sales technique and the techniques and value I bring to my customers have made me successful in my sales position. Here are some examples of what works for me. Pick a few to try and see the results for yourself:

- Be on time to an appointment. Call if you are going to be a few minutes late.

- When you walk in, smile and laugh, the assistant may have more rank than you realize.

- Be sincere and have fun when you walk into an appointment.

- Never slam your competitors, they are trying to make a living too.

- Work anytime and be available anytime. Clients appreciate your working with them when they work, often late at night or early mornings.

- Help train the staff on new products, shoulder to shoulder, on their timetable.

- No matter the size of the customer always give 120%

- Return every call on that day no matter the time

- Return emails, daily and on that day even if you have to work late

- Pay special attention to detail.

- Always give answers to what is asked. Be specific and answer questions directly.

- Bend over backwards for your customer. Research necessary information if asked to do so.

- Always follow through on promises to provide more information.

- Never lie to a customer. Truth is always the best avenue.

- Ask open ended questions of your customers: How is your business doing? What can I do to make you more successful?

- Listen to your customer when they speak. Don't try to talk over them.

I hope you find these tips helpful, as they have helped me to be a success.

Michael Healey
Hillyard, Inc.
Cell: (585) 208-3671
Office: (585) 924-2820

Be Unique by Erica Czop

One of the best pieces of advice I can give to anyone starting their career, is to be unique. We are each our own individual person and you need to embrace that. When you have a passion about what you are selling, the dialogue will just happen naturally. It won't feel like work! When it doesn't feel like work, you will have the most fun. When you are having fun, your unique personality will shine through. Whatever the service or product you that sell, the buyer is only going to remember the uniqueness of you or your company. Find a way to be remembered.

I noticed that every time I do a presentation for a potential client that they look at my hands. Wanting to look professional, I decided that a traditional French manicure would be the best thing for me. Then I discovered that you can have different colors for your fingernail tips. (A French manicure is white on the tips; as it tends to look more natural.) After finding this out I decided to have my nail tech mix a special color just for me. She made me my favorite shade of pink. Now you may be saying to yourself, "You have pink nails, good for you, how does that help me?" My nails have helped me get my foot, or should I say nail, in the door. They make me stand out. One of my potential clients said to me, "I have two girls at home that would love your nails! We should talk."

When you are uniquely yourself you will sell. By creating a signature look, you instantly have something to talk about with people, and it helps to break the ice. People get so nervous when they sell, but if you can have a little fun it makes it easier on you and the potential client. An external expression of your uniqueness, such as my nails, makes it easier to find a safe common ground with a potential client. Finding common ground is often the start to making a sale. I may have had nothing in common with the gentleman who commented on my nails, but he could relate to me because I reminded him of his daughters. By asking a few questions about them, I was able to open him up, and make my sale.

When identifying what you will do to make yourself stand out, be sure that it is still within the realm of professionalism. Your image is important, but you can have a little fun with it too. Be your unique wonderful self, and watch the sales come rolling in.

Passion by Erica Czop

Passion is one of the crucial elements that they, unfortunately, do not teach in college. Stop and ask yourself, "What am I passionate about?" All too often people will say, "I don't care what I do, as long as I can make money." This idea may get you through the beginning of your career path or business, but let me tell you something: If you want to be successful, you need to start getting to know what your passions are. By knowing what your passions are, you will forever exceed your wildest dreams.

I used to stare at the clouds and think to myself, "I just want to make money. Nothing else matters." I was unaware of my fundamental talents in the beginning. I skipped around to a couple of jobs and was not finding success easily. This was tough for me since I had always excelled at my jobs. It wasn't until I looked back at my life, and thought "Where am I going? What do I want in life? Why am I not able to make ends meet?" I was a far cry from where I pictured myself being. Around that same time some members of my family began getting sick, and were hospitalized. It was hard for me to juggle between hospital visits and work at the same time (I had a very competitive job at that point). I thought to myself, "My work pales in comparison to the value and time that I want to give to my family." This was when I started to view things very differently. I took some steps back to reflect: How could I learn, grow, and still feel like I am contributing to society? I wanted to love what I was doing, and balance time between family and work. I finally had my ahah moment. I decided I was going to work for myself, and the rest is history. I have started my life and am now working towards being home 100% of my time. I am doing this by selling products that I love, and helping women with similar goals to mine achieve them. I am getting up in the morning with a smile on my face, and making money to live my dreams. All of this is possible because I made the choice to incorporate my strengths and my passions. When you love what you are doing everything else seems to fall into place.

Erica Czop
Direct Sales
ekkane5@gmail.com

Give It Away by Kevin Krietzberg

When I was selling for my hot sauce business, I had a sales commercial to get me in the door. I would say, "I have a new snack. A wasabi peanut crunchy! Bite into it and get a burst of heat for about 30 seconds, and then it goes away."

My target audience was specialty shops and gift shops. The store owner would try a sample and I would time them to see how long the heat lasted in their mouth. They thought this wasabi peanut was great. On my way out I would leave them samples for everyone. I would give them literature on my product, along with a few other products that I had to offer. I was trying to get my foot in the door with one amazing product and interest them in other products. I knew I had to grab their attention quick. If I tried to sell them all of my products at once, I would have overwhelmed them and probably never heard from them again. I found that offering them a sample was the best way to go. They tried the product and then told their friends. The more people they told, the busier I got. Yes I had to give a small amount of my product away, but the return was well worth it. I was not paying for advertising; I was using word of mouth to get business.

Kevin Krietzberg
Midnight Janitorial Inc.
Kevin@midnightjanitorial.com

What Works for You?

As you read each of these stories, I hope you get a better idea of what sales means to you. Everyone has different opinions of what it means to them, your job is to take a piece from each of them, and find what works for you.

7
The Many Ways to Say Thank You

When I first started my business, I was given invaluable advice: when someone gives you a compliment, simply say "Thank you." No additional words are necessary. For me, this was difficult. I always thought that I had to justify compliments like, "I love your shoes!" I felt the need to explain where they came from, how much I paid for them, and how long I've owned them. The lesson hit home for me when I was out at an event and another woman complimented me on my necklace. Well, of course, I had to go into a ten-minute explanation about how I bought it at a garage sale and how it matched the jacket I bought at Lord & Taylor⁰. She made the comment, "Why do women feel the need to explain everything?" That hit home for me. I started to notice that I did explain everything. I decided that if I didn't just say thank you, I would pinch myself. I can assure you that after about the tenth time of pinching myself, the pain got through to my brain and it became easier to say thank you and not another word.

Handwritten Thank You Notes

After you meet with a potential client, send them a handwritten thank you note. Regardless of whether or not you think you will close the deal, send them a note thanking them for their time. No one does this anymore so this will make you stand out. If the job has more than one company bidding on it, and all things are equal, who do you think is going to stand out? The potential client is also more likely to tell other people about your note. These will be more people who hear about your company. This is the kind of word-of-mouth advertising that you are looking for. Include a business card in your note so that they will have a card to give to friends when they tell them about you.

New Clients

After you land the account, send your new client a small gift as a thank you. For women, I like to send Godiva[a] chocolates or these great candles that I buy from a friend's son. He has a learning disability, and by purchasing the candles from him I get to help support his business. My new client gets a great gift and I help out a friend. For men, I give a gift certificate to a local restaurant. Again, include your business card in the note. You can never give away too many business cards.

Let's take a moment to talk about what to do when you see a current or potential client in a print publication. Cut out the article and send it to them. Be sure and add a brief note saying that you saw them in XYZ publication. Congratulate them on the article that was written, or the award they may have won. People love seeing themselves in print. By sending this card, you are letting them know that you saw them, and you will once more be in front of the competition. If you'd like to go the extra mile, frame the article and wrap it up as a gift that they can keep on their wall to remember you each time they see it.

Referrals

It's important to send a thank you note when someone gives you a referral. A good friend once asked me what she should do for a client who referred her to a new client. She wanted to know if she should take money off their bill or give them a gift certificate to a restaurant. The problem with taking money off the bill is they don't really see this. People want things they can touch; things they can see. The other problem is that the person who gave the referral may not own the company. By taking money off the bill, they won't get anything. Very few companies give a thank you for referrals. A thank you is a sure way to get people talking about you to other people. If you can find a unique gift, all the better, as it will give them even more to talk about.

Helping Hands

Have you ever met someone for coffee or a meal and felt like you learned some valuable information? Did you thank them? Probably not. They took time out of their day to help you. Take time out of your day to send them a thank you. You can send them a note and a small gift, such as a candle, chocolates, or a great business book that you've recently read. As you can see, it doesn't have to be anything extravagant; the important thing is that you do something to show your appreciation.

Speakers

If it's your job to book the speaker for your organization, have a small thank you gift ready for them after their talk, and include a simple thank you note with the gift. When you attend a seminar, it's a great idea to also send a thank you. Let the speaker know that you enjoyed their talk. You may want to include one or two things that you enjoyed. People love to get positive feedback. Again, be sure and include your business card so that the speaker will now know who you are and what you do. Remember the speaker is talking in front of 100's of people and is seen as an expert. Who do you go to when you need something? You go to the expert! If you stand out, they will remember you and give your name out when asked.

Personalize It

You can have thank you cards printed with your logo on them. Customized gift baskets made with a few items with your company logo on them are also available. For added effect, try customizing the basket with items the person likes. Specialty chocolates make a nice gift. I found a basket company who makes these gourmet chocolate covered apples. They have different kinds, some covered in crushed M&M'S[a] or Heath[a] bar pieces and whenever I have given them as thank you gifts, people couldn't stop talking about them. I even received a referral from the basket company. Sadly, I didn't get the client, but one more person now knows about my business.

Vendors

Vendor appreciation is probably the most overlooked thank you. You may wonder "Why would I ever want to thank someone that I already pay for their products/services? What more do they want?" Just like you want to be told that you are doing a good job, so do they. By showing your appreciation, your vendor will remember you and let you know when prices are going up or inventory is running low. They will have your back.

Employees

Last but not least, you need to thank your employees. These people are your most valuable asset. Without them you would not have a business. There are many ways that you can say thank you:

Group Recognition: Have an employee party around the holidays or in the summer. Make sure you let them know that the reason for the party is that they have been doing a good job all year and that you really appreciate them and want them to know it.

Individual Recognition: An employee-of-the-month program is my favorite. A nice certificate along with a gift card works well. Consider allowing each winner to choose a gift card to their favorite establishment.

Now remember, if you are the recipient of any of these thank you gifts all you have to do is to simply say thank you. You don't have to send a card. (This could get confusing if you sent back a thank you card for their thank you card.)

Timing is Everything

If revenge is a dish best served cold, then thank you is a dish best served piping hot! Whatever way you choose to say thank you, say it as soon as possible. It might be a good idea to have some thank you cards and a few small gifts on hand so that it's easy to send a thank you out as soon as you get back to your office or your car. The longer you wait to say thank you, the bigger the gesture should be. Even a text message is fine start five minutes after the encounter, but a month later it won't make much sense. That being said, a thank you anytime is better than no thank you at all.

8
Hiring and Training Employees

One of the most important things you will do in your business (besides finding clients) is to hire good employees. These employees are on the front line; they are the first people your clients interact with.

Interviews

It's wise to have your human resources person hire your staff. If your company is too small to have an HR department you can outsource this position. There are many companies that do HR work per diem. An HR company is a valuable resource. They will be able to tell you about any new or changed laws, and what questions you can and cannot ask during an interview.

My friend Gail Kendig (P.I.N.K. Inc.) has a few interviewing tips. She says, "Literally thousands of people have had to sit in front of me and go through the tortuous ritual of the dreaded interview. Most people are on their best behavior." She personally calls them the Eddie Haskell candidate. "In the late 50's to 60's Leave It to Beaver's brother had a friend who would "act" differently to the adults in the room, then minutes later with his friends, the *real* Eddie would come out. Unfortunately, this happens all too often in the workplace. Once a new hire starts feeling comfortable, the real person allows themselves to show their true colors and the nightmare for the company begins."

One particular company Gail worked for would do group interviews in order to observe and eliminate some of the Eddie Haskell's right away. Gail says, "You can usually see someone's true colors by just observing them. Pair them together by two's and ask them to take a few minutes to get to know each other. After the allotted time, have each person stand up and introduce and share a little bit about the person that they had met to the group. Right away, this will give you a snapshot to the following:

1. Who paid attention to the instructions

2. If only one person was doing all the talking (there wasn't enough to share about one of the partners)

3. If they were a good listener and able to repeat what they heard

4. If two people start to speak at the same time, you can wait and watch for the person who says "I'm sorry, you go first"

After this type of exercise we would have them do more team-style activities showing us who seemed to be a leader, who was too aggressive verses assertive, who was too passive, and those who were just too shy to represent our company. This is a very brief overview that I am sharing of course. The final portion of the interview is simple. Who picked up after themselves? Even better, who picked up after others? Who put the chairs back under the table? Who stayed to help others? For us this was one of the most important parts of the interview since we were hiring for a service position. Integrity and kindness is much better to see than to read. Ultimately, a resume is not going to give you this information. The best thing to do is observe everything you can and ask lots of performance based questions. Past behavior actually does equal future behavior."

Gail Kendig
P.I.N.K Inc.
gailkendig@gmail.com
www.gailkendig.com

Termination

When the time comes to terminate one of your employees, your HR firm can do this for you as well. Since your HR firm is a neutral party without any emotional involvement, you don't have to worry about them saying the wrong thing. They will write up the termination document; everything will be spelled out, and the terminated employee will sign it. Ayana Williams of Williamsen Consulting suggests that you have a witness present when discussing issues, especially termination, with your employee. If it is just you and the employee in the room, it becomes your word against theirs. With a witness you have someone to back up your claims.

Human Resources

I have an HR company that I use from time to time, and they have saved me from making numerous mistakes. When I need to hire a new employee they interview them for me. At one point I thought that I had the perfect candidate, but oh boy, was I wrong! The HR firm conducted the interview and found out that at her last job, the potential employee had argued with a customer. When they asked her if she would do this again her response was, "Yes, if I know I am right and they are wrong. I have to defend myself." My philosophy is that the customer is always right. You never argue with them. I could have had some serious customer service issues if I had hired her. Considering that it takes five times the amount of money to get a new client than it does to keep a current client happy, the cost of hiring an HR company to conduct interviews was well worth the money to me. It could have cost me a lot more to undo some of the mistakes I might have made.

Define roles

When you get ready to hire new employees, make sure that you have a written job description for each position. Make it as detailed as possible. Hiring new employees is time consuming and costly. You don't want someone quitting because they thought the job they applied for was different from the actual position they received. By clearly defining what you expect of them, there is no question about what you want them to do. You cannot expect them to do a good job if they don't know what is expected of them.

An employee handbook is different from a job description, in that it explains your company policies and procedures, and it applies to all of your employees. However, you may have policies for full-time people that may not apply to part-time workers. Once you have 50 employees, there are policies that you legally have to follow. Check with your local payroll company or HR firm to see what the exact employee number is in your state and what applies to you. For a fee, your payroll or HR firm will create an employee handbook for you. Once complete, you only have to send out an addendum to the handbook to let the employees know of any changes that you wish to make. Make sure you review the handbook with each employee that you hire. Your HR firm can do this for you during employee orientation. After the handbook has been reviewed, the employee should sign a document saying that they have read and understood the content of the handbook. This is your safety net if they later try and come back at you for a policy that they feel is wrong. You can pull out the paper they signed and show it to them. Keep a copy of this signed document in the employee's file.

An employee file, or personnel file, is basically a folder that contains all information about a particular employee. The employee's application, tax forms, as well as any certifications that they have earned will go into this folder. According to Ayana Williams of Williamsen Consulting, you need to be careful with these files. They must be kept in a locked filling cabinet. You also need to keep a separate folder for all your employees' I-9 forms. These do not go into their personal file. The best advice that Ayana says she can offer people is: 1) Document everything: any reprimands, rewards promised, and issues that happened with your employees. If you go to court it is better to have too much information vs. having too little; and 2) When in doubt, contact an HR professional. It is easier to pay a small fee upfront and do things right vs. paying lawyers, and fines later. The judge will not take the excuse, "I didn't know I was doing anything wrong." Ignorance is a costly excuse.

Hire Smart People

It is smart to hire people who are smarter than you. If they have a lot of experience in the field you are hiring for, snap them up. There will be times when you have to rely on their experience to close a deal or to solve a problem. You may not know to ask certain questions, and you can use their knowledge to your advantage. I was initially hesitant to hire "experts" for fear that they would leave my company for a better position. Although, I wanted them to grow with my company, I often couldn't afford to pay them what they were worth. After talking with my financial planner, I found out that I could offer them a bonus (a nice sum of money) in five or ten years if they were still with my company. Who doesn't want to receive a big chunk of money for being loyal and doing a good job year after year? Talk with your financial advisor for more details about how this works.

Non-Compete/Non-Disclosure

A non-disclosure agreement (NDA) protects you and your clients. It simply states that your employees will not repeat anything that they see or hear while on the job. Your clients will feel better knowing that your employee understands not to say anything about any sensitive information that they may come across. Each employee should be required to sign a NDA. A happy employee can quickly become angry and vindictive if they feel that they have been wronged in some way. They may feel tempted to share your company secrets with others, however, once they have signed the NDA, they are legally bound to not repeat anything that they see or know. It is better to be safe than sorry.

If you are going to be sharing company secrets with your employees, you may want to have a non-compete contract. This is a contract that states that the other party cannot start a business that competes with yours for a certain period of time. You can stipulate however many years you want, but it's usually anywhere from five to ten years.

Training Your Employees

Now that you have hired your employees you need to train them. Everyone learns differently. Even the way you speak and act is perceived differently. Seven percent of people are influenced by the words we say, 38% by the tone of our voice, and 55% are influenced by what our body is doing as we are speaking.

When training a new employee you first need to understand how that person learns. A good trainer will use different methods, such as activities or discussions, to discover how the person learns. Twenty percent of people learn through reading, 20% from what they hear, 30% from what they see, and 50% from what they see and hear.

As we are learning, we go through three phases of processing. The first is paying attention. As the trainer you need to get the trainee to understand why the training is important to them and why they should work hard to master this skill. Perhaps their job is depending on it, or they will get a raise, or move up the company ladder once they have these skills. When people understand what is in it for them, they are more likely to work harder. They have a vested interest in doing a good job.

The next phase is the information phase; what are you actually showing them? This is where knowing the difference between the various ways people learn will help you. Mix it up. If you just stand there in a monotone voice explaining what to do, you will lose people. Remember, 50% learn from what they see AND hear. You can use visual guides, written words, or live action. Just make sure you keep it interesting.

The third phase talks about our prior experiences. The trainee is going to take what you are teaching them and compare it to what they have previously experienced. Many of us have probably heard, "That's not how I was taught." As the trainer, you want to allow people to express their beliefs and find a way to bring their past experiences together with the present methods being taught.

Next, the trainee makes conclusions about what they have been taught, and they come to understand what the information means. Since everyone learns differently, it is the trainer's job to guide the trainee and offer help and support to learn the new material.

Once the training is done, the learner will decide if the information they learned can be used. They will experience and decide whether to accept the training or reject it.

To recap, the phases of learning are as follows:

- Paying Attention
- Information
- Prior Experience Integration
- Conclusion
- Acceptance/Rejection

When I am training a new person I first show them a training video. This video shows them exactly how I want them to clean each area. Then I show them how to clean by watching me physically do it. I then watch them clean that particular area. This is where I can correct any mistakes as they go along. I will also ask them questions such as: What's next? How do you clean this or where does the garbage go? When they are done with the visual training they are given a written manual that explains in detail how things are done. They are tested on this manual every six months. They have now seen it and read about it. My thought behind testing them is that people become complacent after a while. I like them to stay fresh and on point.

As I said earlier, everyone learns differently. One person may go through the phases of learning faster than another person. Adjust your training to the employee's needs. Never make assumptions about your potential employee, or coworker. Everyone has different skills that they bring to the table. You are forming a TEAM of employees that works well together. **T**ogether **E**veryone **A**chieves **M**ore.

Employees Not Getting Along

There may be times when your employees will not all get along. As the owner, it is your responsibility to have them work out their issues without taking sides. For instance, you don't want to alienate the new person just because everyone else has been working there since the beginning. You also don't want to judge a person too quickly. Take time to find out what the issue is and how it can be resolved so that everyone is happy. My friend Gail has an interesting story about a coworker and how she could have lost out by judging her too quickly.

"At some point, years ago, I was working at a major corporation and climbing toward the corporate glass ceiling. My company had two divisions, Corporate and Industrial. I was an employee in the corporate side of the company, maintaining, building, and problem solving for our clients. After being there for a few years and fighting for each raise it was important for me to capture every opportunity for growth. It was brought to my attention that the fairly new 26-year-old, young woman was coming from the industrial side to the corporate side to become our Supervisor. I was fuming! Who was SHE and what could she *possibly* teach me? I believe I was about five big years older. I wasn't very kind, but I wasn't mean either. I just 'did my thing' and stayed out of the way. At the same time, we hired another peer to our division. This new person and I didn't always get along because she saw everything as a joke. She didn't take anything seriously and it was quite annoying, especially when it came to solving problems. It drove me crazy. We occasionally had a few words exchanged. Our new 26-year-old boss said this was becoming a problem. So she sat us down and told us that we were not to leave this room until we could get along. It was torture. Me and this crazy woman left alone...I wanted to strangle at least one of them!

As it turns out my 26-year-old supervisor was brilliant, and from that day on I continued to learn about her and from her. She was the youngest of her siblings and her parents were in there 60's and 70's. She was highly educated and qualified. She ended up being the best supervisor and one of the most powerful mentors I have ever had. You know what they say, 'don't judge a book by its cover.'"

Your employees will become one of your most valuable assets. Take advantage of every opportunity to train and guide them properly. Use the resources that you will acquire to hire the right people.

9

Raving Fan, Person to Confide In Find One Person to Confide In

When you start your business, you probably won't know a lot of people or businesses. (Even if you do, this chapter can still help you.) The first thing you want to do is to find one person (you may or may not already know this person) whom you can trust. This person has to "have your back" as I like to say. This will be the one person whom you can confide in when your business isn't doing well or when things get crazy. We have all been there, when you are really upset and want to send a nasty email. Rather than burn any bridges by sending out a nasty note too soon, you can vent your frustration in an email to the person that you have chosen to confide in. Let them be the person who is reasonable. They are removed from the situation, and will not be as emotional as you are. They will look at the email and offer to rewrite it with you. Even still, you should wait at least 24 hours before you hit send. This will give you time to calm down, and reevaluate why you are upset. Or as is often the case, the situation may have naturally resolved itself by then.

You will also use this person to bounce ideas around with. Sometimes you may think that you have a brilliant idea and when you start talking about it, your friend starts to poke holes in it. You realize that maybe it wasn't the best idea. The good thing is that you didn't tell anyone else. On the other hand, perhaps you have a good idea and your friend can help you make it a bit better. When I was writing this book, I would show the chapters to my good friend Lisa Riggi. When I thought I had the best ideas for this book, Lisa would read them, and very nicely tell me that I wasn't getting my point across like I thought I was. She could tell where I wanted to go, but it just wasn't happening. I needed her to tell me that I was rambling or saying the word "so" too much. I have the bad habit of putting the word "so" in front of every other sentence. Had I just sent my ideas to the publisher as they were, well you probably wouldn't be reading this book right now. I trusted Lisa to tell me the truth, and to not laugh at my ideas.

There are going to be days when you want to quit your business, and your friend is there to pump you back up. Even the most accomplished people have their moments of weakness when they start to doubt themselves. I asked Lisa numerous times if she was sure I was doing the right thing by writing this book. What if no one wanted to read it? What if it didn't sell? Lisa just kept on being my cheerleader, along with a few of my other friends (Heather Smith, Sue Kastan, and Kathy Porter to name a few). These were people that I knew I could count on to cheer me up. I am also always there for them as well. Make sure you return the favor to your friend when they are in need.

Accountability Partner/Accountability Group

An accountability partner holds you accountable for the goals and actions that you commit to doing. You are more likely to do the things you set out to do if you have to face someone and say, "I didn't get so and so done." Have you ever had to tell someone you didn't do something you said you would do? I bet you felt a little guilty. There are a few women I meet with once a month. We discuss things that are happening in our businesses, and issues we might be dealing with. At the end of every meeting we set goals that we want to achieve by the next meeting. At one point, I had this book almost finished except that I just needed to go back in and make a few minor changes. Do you think I could get it done? Nope, I kept putting it off. I was so close to the finish line and I just kept procrastinating. I finally brought this up to my women's accountability group, and decided to make it my goal for the next month. I now had a reason to finish up; I didn't want to disappoint them. I didn't want to have to face them the next month and say that I had slacked off for no reason. Sometimes you need that little extra push to get it done. Your accountability partner is also going to be your cheerleader. They are going to be the one who boosts your spirits when business isn't going so well and when you say you want to quit and get a "job." This happens to all of us. Business isn't so great; you are struggling to make it and you just want to give up. They will be there for you. Your friends will be the ones to talk you off the ledge. Deep down you know you don't want to work for someone else. You want to be your own boss.

Vent Before You Send

This is such an important concept, that it bears mentioning again. Don't get caught in the trap of anger. As I said earlier, if you are angry at someone, before you send that letter or email or before you make that phone call, talk to your friend; vent to them. Explain what you plan to say. Take their advice when they tell you not to use such harsh language. If you send it while you are mad, you will only regret it later. Once something has been sent, it is out there forever. You can never take it back. Don't burn any bridges. The business community is smaller than you think. Word will get out of your actions. You may find it more difficult to grow your business, especially if no one wants to help you. A lot of times the way you perceive something can be a simple misunderstanding. Feel free to ask questions, and then let the person know what you perceived them to be saying.

Have you ever heard of the telephone game? How the game works is that one person tells the person next to them a predetermined sentence. For example, they may use "Johnny has a blue shirt on and is going to the store." You go around the room and each person repeats what they "think they hear." By the time you get to the last person, the sentence is usually completely changed. It may turn out to be "Billy has black shorts on and is going to the hospital." This is how gossip gets started. You don't want anything to do with this. It will come back to bite you. If you are dying to tell someone, tell your friend that you trust to vent to. This way you still get to tell someone and it goes no further.

Remember you have to be there for your friend as well. If your friend has issues, you need to listen and offer your advice. Both of you need to understand that anything you two discuss will not be repeated. Often times, my friend and I will say, "This does not leave the room." We both know that, but a simple reminder helps ease our minds.

Raving Fan

Let's talk again about the concept of the raving fan (Terry introduced us to the raving fan in an earlier chapter). This is the person who goes out and consistently talks you up. They will go out of their way to talk about you. You can have more than one raving fan. A raving fan can be a client, a friend, or someone you met who took an instant liking to you. A raving fan will usually only talk about one person or company at a time, however they will have numerous people or companies that they can talk about. They will decide which one is a good fit for whomever they are talking to at any given time. I love my hairdresser. She does amazing things to my hair without me having to tell her what I want done. I am not going to tell a bald man how great she is. I won't mention her to him because I don't want to offend him. If I just met him, I don't know if he is sensitive about being bald. I would think of another company or person who would best fit his needs. (For more advice on this, refer back to Chapter Six on Sales.)

You want a raving fan, because often times people like to hear from someone other than yourself about how great your company is. If you say this yourself, people may think that you are bragging. If someone else talks about you and your accomplishments then they will just be seen as a satisfied customer. Your raving fan is someone who is aware of your services and can vouch for you. Think about it like this: when you apply for a job, you provide your potential employer with references. These references are just people willing to say that you are a good person. When you hire a contractor you ask for references, because you want to know whom else they have worked with. This is your raving fan; your reference person. Choose this person wisely. Their reputation is going to be attached to yours. You don't want someone who is known for being unethical running around town talking about how you two are such good friends and what a wonderful job you do.

Sadly, people will judge you based on who your acquaintances are. Think about it: when you meet someone new, you instantly judge them. You don't want someone to judge you based on this person's reputation. When I was giving a bid a few years back, the company I wanted to work for had heard that I used to be associated with another company (we will call them ABC Company. Although at one time we had been pretty good friends with ABC Company, we decided to part ways after a long relationship because we couldn't agree on how we should be running our businesses. Well, this new company asked me if I was still working with ABC Company. I immediately said no, and that we had to part ways due to an unethical situation. Since winning the Rochester Business Ethics award and the (National) American Business Ethics award, our company decided that we could not partner with a company that did not share our same values. After a short pause the new company said "Good, we are glad to hear that! You can start cleaning for us on the first of the month." I often wonder if I still would have gotten the new client if I had told them that I was still associated with ABC Company. They had obviously heard something bad about ABC Company and that we were connected to them. I guess I will never know, but I am thankful that I chose to do what was right for my company. Choose your raving fan, and who you are going to partner with carefully to avoid any future regret.

Get Your Own Raving Fan

The question now becomes: How do you get a raving fan? Do you just go up to someone and ask them? You could, but that may seem like a forced conversation. Instead, it is better to simply do good things for your clients and friends and go beyond what is expected of you (refer to section on Customer Service in Chapter Four). Once people start to see how great you are, they will want to talk about you to others. You may also want to become a raving fan for them; they may or may not reciprocate. This is OK There is a concept in business we mentioned earlier called "pay it forward." This is where you do good things for others and in time, good things will happen to you. Sometimes it works out and other times, it doesn't. I met a guy who did recruiting for different companies. We talked about our companies, exchanged business cards, and did the usual call me if either of our services were ever needed. I didn't speak to him again for about five years. The good thing is that he did remember me and when a need was presented to him, he gave out my name. I got the client! To this day, I have not had an opportunity to give him a referral back. I have given referrals to a lot of other people though, just not to him.

Having many raving fans running around town talking you up is a great thing: 1) it's free advertising; and 2) people/companies are more likely to listen to an actual person who has used your services. They have real experience to talk about and are not just an ad that you created to say whatever you want. Here is a real life person giving a real testimonial. Potential clients can ask them questions to get a better understanding of how they feel, how they were treated, and so on. Raving fans will give an honest answer, not a predetermined sales pitch, because they have no real stake in whether or not someone buys. They are just a happy customer, who feels that they have received a good service and want to share it with others.

10
Plan for the Unexpected/ Get It In Writing

Of all the concepts covered in this book, the most important by far may well be to plan for the unexpected. When I first started my business, I set it up so that if I was removed from it unexpectedly, everything would still run smoothly. As you can guess, the unexpected did happen. I went to the hospital with what I thought was an asthma attack. Well, I awoke four days later, and have no memory of what happened. I had no time to give directions to my employees. They had to do things as they normally would, but without their leader. This was no fire drill. They had to run the business as if all was well. I would test them many times over the next few years with my frequent trips to the hospital. I never was able to give them any notice. I am proud to say that my staff all stepped up and did whatever had to be done. Since I had a plan, there was no confusion. The good thing about my plan is that I know I can take a nice vacation whenever I want and have no worries. They had already been tested and passed with flying colors.

Worst Case

When I say plan for the unexpected, I mean plan for the worst case scenario. If you couldn't communicate with your staff, would your company still be able to function? I know the chances of this happening are slim; but do you really want to take that chance? In school we often practiced fire drills. The school never planned for any actual fire, but we practiced just as if the school were burning down. We all knew what to do. No one was running around asking for directions. You may think that I am being a bit extreme here. After all, what is the worst thing that could happen? I don't know. Did anyone plan for 9/11 to happen? Does anyone plan for their home office to burn down with all of your important client files on your computer? Perhaps you should have backed everything up on a removable hard drive or an off-site backup system. The plan does not have to be some elaborate idea. It can be as simple as knowing who does payroll if you are not around. Who would do your employee schedule if you were unable to? My hope is that you never need your backup plan. But won't you rest easier at night knowing that you have this security blanket? I sure do. My employees do as well. They are well trained in what should happen. Having a plan reduces employee stress so they can do a better job without the added pressure of uncertainty.

Cross Training

Another way that I have planned for uncertainty is to train employees to do multiple jobs. I was worried that if someone called in sick or quit, who would do their job? I went a step further by making a list that is available to someone that tells them who knows what jobs. For instance, I showed someone else how to do the schedules. This was an important area for me to have a backup. Also, by giving the schedules to another manager, I no longer have to do them. I still check them for errors, but I am able to better spend my time doing other things that make me money. Basically, make sure that any jobs you do yourself, someone else knows how to do as well.

You might also consider hiring a bookkeeper to do some of your work. Again, remember the more jobs you can delegate, the more free time you have to use as you wish.

Business Continuity Planning

Here are some tips from Sue Kastan of Kastan Consulting about the top things that you should plan for:

Business owners need to think about how they will handle many different types of disruptions including interruptions to their information technology, workplace, and workforce. In very general terms information technology is any technology that helps to produce, manipulate, store, communicate, and/or disseminate information. It includes desktop and laptop computers, flash drives (also called thumb drives, etc), smartphones, cell phones, and PDA's as well as firewalls, servers, printers, and many other things.

With so much under the "information technology" umbrella, planning for a disruption can be overwhelming. An easy place to start is to protect your technology from loss and theft. For example, laptops should be locked away when not in use. Another easy thing to do is to install anti-virus and anti-spyware on your computer and keep them up to date. In addition, data on laptops, desktops, smartphones, etc. should be backed up regularly. Backups should be stored in a separate location if possible. At a minimum, the backups should be stored in a fireproof and waterproof safe. If you don't live in an area that floods regularly, you may wonder why your safe also needs to be waterproof. What happens when the firemen put out that fire with those big hoses? Regardless, backup files should be tested regularly to ensure that the backup is valid.

The next disruption to consider is a disruption to your workplace. One of the most common workplace disruptions is a power outage. Without power, phone systems, computers, production machines, electronic locks, and elevators may not work. Can work continue in your facility if the power goes out? If you have a generator, do you have enough fuel to run the critical operations until power is restored?

Last but not least, consider how you would handle a disruption to your workforce. Employees are one of a company's most important assets. Without your workforce, your work cannot get done. Employers should plan for the loss of a key individual as well as the loss of a group of individuals. For example, if the president of the company suddenly takes ill, can operations go on without him? If the entire billing department falls sick for two weeks, can bills go out to maintain the cash flow? One of the most effective ways to protect your workforce, your workplace, and your information technology is to have a plan in place to handle disruptions that may arise. Here are five basic steps to writing a disaster recovery or business continuity plan:

1. **Perform an assessment** of your business starting with the things already discussed in this chapter. For the best results, hire a professional to do your assessment. They have experience evaluating situations and may unearth serious risks that you have not considered.

2. **Determine the most important processes in your business.** These will be the things that need to be handled first when things go wrong.

3. **Write your plan.** This part is important. A plan that exists only in someone's head is a waste. If you don't know exactly what to put in the plan or do not have time to do the plan yourself, invest the money to have someone write the plan for you.

4. **Train everyone on the plan.** Training can be as simple as a poster or as elaborate as a video presentation depending on the message and the audience.

5. **Test the plan.** It is during testing that problems can be found and corrected. In a tabletop test, key individuals sit around a table and talk over a proposed problem. During the discussion, procedures, documentation, and checklists are reviewed for accuracy. Information technology tests help to ensure that your information and that your computers work as intended.

There are many reasons to have a plan. Having a disaster recovery or business continuity plan can provide both business owner and employees peace of mind. Lucy, a networking friend, mentioned that her company actually had a disaster. The business owner had the foresight to have a plan in place. As a result, the office staff had an alternate location where they reported to work the next day. Lucy remembers that it was a little unnerving to be working in a different location, but it felt good to know that business could go on as usual for the most part.

In addition to the peace of mind for the owner and employees, there are also financial reasons for having a plan. It is almost always cheaper to implement a plan proactively than to respond reactively. Lost productivity and emergency service calls add up quickly. Lastly, having a plan allows a faster recovery from a disruption which may enable a business to reduce the amount of insurance it carries.

Susan Kastan
Kastan Consulting, LLC
www.kastanconsulting.com
(585) 734-0804

Get It In Writing

One of the things most often overlooked is to get things in writing. A good friend of mine was trying to help a friend of hers to launch a product. We will call it product X to protect their identities. My friend, whom will call Sandy, and her friend, we will call Trina. Sandy started selling product X to a couple of businesses. Sandy told Trina what she had sold, expecting to get a check for her sales. Instead, Trina offered her some products as payment. Sandy was counting on getting money to pay some of her bills. The product she was being offered was of no use to her. The problem was that neither one of them had discussed compensation. If they had written down what each party was expecting, no one would have walked away upset. There would have been no confusion. Each party would have gone into the agreement with clearly defined expectations.

When you are hired by a new client, you should clearly define what you are going to give them. What services are you going to provide? You also want to include what the client is going to provide and most importantly, when will they will pay you.

If you are going to hire employees, be sure to clearly define what you expect of them by writing down an explicit job description. You can't expect them to do a good job if they don't know what the job is. By clearly defining their role, they are able to do a better job for you.

When I started my business, my husband was working for me. All we did was fight. Neither one of us knew what we were supposed to do. One day we sat down and clearly defined what each of us was supposed to do. He was much better at paying bills than I was. I was much better with the employees. While follow up is not a strong suit of mine, my husband is quite skilled in that area. We decided that I would not be able to give an employee a raise until I had discussed with him why I felt that an employee should get a raise. In the same instance, if my husband wanted to fire an employee, he would have to come to me and explain why he wanted them fired. This is just one example of how we defined our roles. A good piece of advice I can give married couples or people who plan to have partners in their business, is to sit down and define your roles. You will stay together longer!

When you hire a service, ensure you have in writing what they are going to do for you. Just as you want to define your role for a new client, you are the new client in this situation. I decided I wanted my website to have pictures of my employees on it. The first thing I did was to make sure to have my employees sign a contract allowing me rights to their photograph so that they would not be able to come back and sue me for using their photo. Remember, when it comes to money you can't trust people. You may be thinking I don't have anything for them to sue me for. They won't be thinking about that now. It's when you start making millions is when they starting coming around.

When you go to rent your commercial property, get everything writing. Be sure to include things like how long the lease is and who is responsible for snow and garbage removal. Make it as detailed as possible with your expectations clearly spelled out. After you sign the lease you can't go back a month later and say that you are not happy with the bill you received for garbage removal. Had you clearly stated this in the lease agreement, you would have known who was going to be responsible. As a business owner, you have enough unexpected issues arising; you don't want to add more by cutting corners and not taking the time to clearly define everything.

Employee Write-ups

If you decide to have employees, it is imperative to document everything that happens. If they are late, write it down. If they are not following your rules, document it. If an employee decides that you fired them unfairly and takes you to court, you need documentation of the events that happened. Have the employee sign off that they agree that they did what you are saying they did. You lawyer can only help you if you have given them proper evidence. By getting everything in writing, you are protecting yourself and your business. A lawyer once told me that you can never over document. It is better to go in with too much information than to be scrambling after the fact. This really applies to everyone starting a business or working in business. If you are unsure of how to properly document, or what you should document, contact your local HR firm. They can help you navigate this touchy subject. You can even hire an HR firm to give the write up to the employee. I tend to have a temper when I feel people are disrespecting me, or giving me an attitude. I have hired an HR firm to give all my write ups to my employees. This saves me from perhaps getting sued for my improper attitude. Remember that you usually write an employee up because they are doing something improper. Do you think they are going to be happy? Doubtful, and how do you think you would react to them giving you attitude? Better to pay a small fee and let someone else handle the situation.

Conclusion

We have covered a lot here. We started out by discussing your plan for your new business, who your clients will be, and how you will finance your startup. We went on to talk about the importance of networking, where to network and how often to network. We discussed how to dress your best, and the all important rules to following up with potential clients.

We touched on setting goals that are realistic, and how to reward yourself. I think Heather Smith got the best reward, with her trip to Africa. It's important to visualize yourself achieving your goals, but more importantly, you have to take action.

Some of the ways to take action are to work on branding yourself. What message is it that you want to send out? What types of information do you want to put on your website and in your brochure? After all, these things are extensions of your brand, and must all be cohesive.

Once you have your brand, you need to start getting your name out there. Perhaps you will become an expert speaker or writer. (Hey I did it, anyone can!) You can apply for awards to help distinguish your company from your competition. When you win you can send out press releases letting everyone know how great you are doing.

I've given you a look into the world of a few different sales people. Take a little from each one of them and create your own unique sales style.

Remember to thank your employees and clients. Without them you have no business. Don't forget the people along the way who will help you grow your business with either information or leads.

We have even touched on the subject of hiring and, unfortunately, firing employees. When hiring people, or seeking guidance, always choose people smarter than you. They have all the experience you need in that particular field, so that you can tap into their intelligence and grow your business. Training is going to be a very important part of your business. If you don't show your employees the proper way to do something, you cannot expect them to do it the way you want it done.

Once you start to meet all these great people, find one you can confide in. There will come a point in your business, when you just need to vent. Go to your friend and vent until you feel better. Be there for that friend if they need to vent to you.

And finally, always plan for the unexpected. Life can be going along great and wham you get hit with the curve ball. You can't plan for everything, but you can be prepared. Change will happen in your business; don't be afraid of it, learn and grow from it.

This is a lot of information to absorb. Keep this book handy as your reference guide. Make lots of notes in the margin. My last piece of advice for you is to never stop learning. Someone once told me that there are no mistakes in life, just lessons learned. Seek out mentors and professionals that will keep you learning about your business.

Go out in the world armed with the knowledge that you can and will succeed in your dream business! Find your wisdom in a traffic jam.

Angella Luyk

Contributors

I would like to thank the following contributing writers. They are more than business associates to me; they are my friends. Each has added their own personal stories to this book; I hope you enjoyed reading about them.

Emily Carpenter
WhizBang! Web Solutions LLC
www.whizbangweb.com
(585) 288-7254

Erica Czop
Direct Sales
ekkane5@gmail.com

Jerry Elman
Schoen Place Auto
www.schoenplaceauto.com
(585) 381-1970

Terry Glasbergen
Glasbergen Marketing Services
tglasbergen@gmail.com
(888) 945-7779

Michael Healey
Hillyard, Inc.
Cell: (585) 208-3671
Office: (585) 924-2820

Susan Kastan
Kastan Consulting, LLC
www.kastanconsulting.com
(585) 734-0804

Gail Kendig
P.I.N.K Inc.
gailkendig@gmail.com
www.gailkendig.com

Kevin Kluth
Pinnacle Cleaning
www.rochestercarpetcare.com
www.rochesterrugcleaning.com
(585) 309-1990

Kevin Krietzberg
Midnight Janitorial Inc.
Kevin@midnightjanitorial.com

Heather A. Smith, LUTCF, CLTC
Financial Architects/MassMutual
heathersmith@finsvcs.com
www.financialarchitectsupstate.com

BUY A SHARE OF THE FUTURE IN YOUR COMMUNITY

These certificates make great holiday, graduation and birthday gifts that can be personalized with the recipient's name. The cost of one S.H.A.R.E. or one square foot is $54.17. The personalized certificate is suitable for framing and will state the number of shares purchased and the amount of each share, as well as the recipient's name. The home that you participate in "building" will last for many years and will continue to grow in value.

Here is a sample SHARE certificate:

THIS CERTIFIES THAT

YOUR NAME HERE

HAS INVESTED IN A HOME FOR A DESERVING FAMILY

1985-2010

TWENTY-FIVE YEARS OF BUILDING FUTURES
IN OUR COMMUNITY ONE HOME AT A TIME

1200 SQUARE FOOT HOUSE @ $65,000 = $54.17 PER SQUARE FOOT
This certificate represents a tax deductible donation. It has no cash value.

YES, I WOULD LIKE TO HELP!

I support the work that Habitat for Humanity does and I want to be part of the excitement! As a donor, I will receive periodic updates on your construction activities but, more importantly, I know my gift will help a family in our community realize the dream of homeownership. **I would like to SHARE in your efforts against substandard housing in my community!** *(Please print below)*

PLEASE SEND ME _____ SHARES at $54.17 EACH = $ $_____

In Honor Of: _____

Occasion: *(Circle One)*   *HOLIDAY*   *BIRTHDAY*   *ANNIVERSARY*

     OTHER: _____

Address of Recipient: _____

Gift From: _____ *Donor Address:* _____

Donor Email: _____

I AM ENCLOSING A CHECK FOR $ $_____ **PAYABLE TO HABITAT FOR HUMANITY OR** PLEASE CHARGE MY VISA OR MASTERCARD *(CIRCLE ONE)*

Card Number _____ Expiration Date: _____

Name as it appears on Credit Card _____ Charge Amount $ _____

Signature _____

Billing Address _____

Telephone # Day _____ Eve _____

PLEASE NOTE: Your contribution is tax-deductible to the fullest extent allowed by law.
Habitat for Humanity • P.O. Box 1443 • Newport News, VA 23601 • 757-596-5553
www.HelpHabitatforHumanity.org

Printed in the USA
CPSIA information can be obtained
at www.ICGtesting.com
JSHW082213140824
68134JS00014B/609

9 781600 379765